G000078034

CREDITS

1732011

191984

221084

AUX SYS

SYSTEM DESIGN
NATHAN DOWDELL

LINE DEVELOPMENT
SAM WEBB

RED ALERT DESIGN
MARK LATHAM AND SAM WEBB

WRITING
CHRIS MCCARVER, ANDY PEREGRINE,
JACK GEIGER, JOHN SNEAD, SAM WEBB,
AND MARK LATHAM

EDITING
SCOTT PEARSON, JIM JOHNSON,
AND MIKE BRUNTON

PROOFREADING
MATEUSZ PŁOSZCZYCA

COVER ARTWORK
ELI MAFFEI

PHOTOGRAPHY
SALWA AZAR

INTERNAL ARTWORK
MICHAL E. CROSS, WAYNE MILLER,
DAVID METLESITS, VINCENT LAIK,
ADAM "MOJO" LEBOWITZ, GRZEGORZ
PEDRYCZ, RODRIGO GONZALEZ,
NICK GREENWOOD, ÁNGEL ALONSO
MIGUEL, JACK KAISER, ADAM LANE,
ALAIN RIVARD, AND TOMA FEIZO GAS

ART DIRECTION
SAM WEBB AND JIM JOHNSON

GRAPHIC DESIGN
MATTHEW COMBEN

LAYOUT
MICHAL E. CROSS

INDEX
BILL HERON

PRODUCED BY
CHRIS BIRCH

PUBLISHING ASSISTANT
SALWA AZAR

OPERATIONS MANAGER
GARRY HARPER

PRODUCTION MANAGER
STEVE DALDRY

STUDIO MANAGER
JON WEBB

RED ALERT PLAYTESTING
JAVIER ANGERIZ-CABURRASI, JAMES BARRY,
FEDERICO SOHNS, AND JON WEBB

COMMUNITY SUPPORT
LLOYD GYAN

FOR CBS STUDIOS
BILL BURKE, JOHN VAN CITTERS,
MARIAN CORDRY, VERONICA HART,
BRIAN LADY, AND KEITH LOWENADLER

MŌDIPHIÜS™
ENTERTAINMENT
2d20™

Published by Modiphius Entertainment Ltd.
2nd Floor, 39 Harwood Road, London, SW6 4QP, England.
Printed by Grafik Media Produktionsmanagement, Köln

INFO@MODIPHIUS.COM
WWW.MODIPHIUS.COM
STARTREK.COM

Modiphius Entertainment Product Number: MUH051064
ISBN: 978-1-910132-88-3

The 2d20 system and Modiphius Logos are copyright Modiphius
Entertainment Ltd. 2018. All 2d20 system text is copyright Modiphius
Entertainment Ltd. Any unauthorised use of copyrighted material is illegal.
Any trademarked names are used in a fictional manner; no infringement
is intended. This is a work of fiction. Any similarity with actual people and
events, past or present, is purely coincidental and unintentional except for
those people and events described in an historical context. ™ & © 2018
CBS Studios Inc. © 2018 Paramount Pictures Corp. STAR TREK and related
marks and logos are trademarks of CBS Studios inc. All Rights Reserved.

Artwork and graphics © and ™ CBS Studios Inc. All Rights Reserved.,
except the Modiphius Logo which is ™ Modiphius Entertainment Ltd.
This is a work of fiction. Any similarity with actual people and events,
past or present, is purely coincidental and unintentional except for those
people and events described in an historical context.

CHAPTER 01   003

INTRODUCTION

01.10   Breaking the Laws of Physics 004

CHAPTER 02   009

OPERATIONS DIVISION

02.10   Fleet Operations 010
02.20   Starfleet Intelligence 016
02.30   Starfleet Corps of Engineers.................................. 023
02.40   Section 31... 029

CHAPTER 03   035

OPERATIONS DIVISION CHARACTERS

03.10   Security School.. 036
03.20   Engineering School.. 044

CHAPTER 04   053

ADVANCED TECHNOLOGY

04.10   Engineering Devices 054
04.20   Starship Systems.. 058
04.30   Experimental Engineering...................................... 061

CHAPTER 05   065

USING THE OPERATIONS DIVISION

05.10   Operations Department Storylines 066
05.20   Engineering Department Storylines........................... 075

CHAPTER 06   083

OPERATIONS PERSONNEL

06.10   Starfleet Intelligence 084
06.20   Starfleet Corps of Engineers.................................. 087
06.30   Starfleet Personnel 090
06.40   Supporting Characters 093

CHAPTER 07   097

RED ALERT

07.10   Rules of Play.. 098
07.20   Starting a Game... 100
07.30   The Battlefield... 108
07.40   Weapons and Equipment 109
07.50   Missions.. 113
07.60   Tokens... 117

Index.. 118

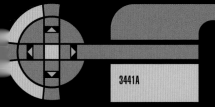

3441A

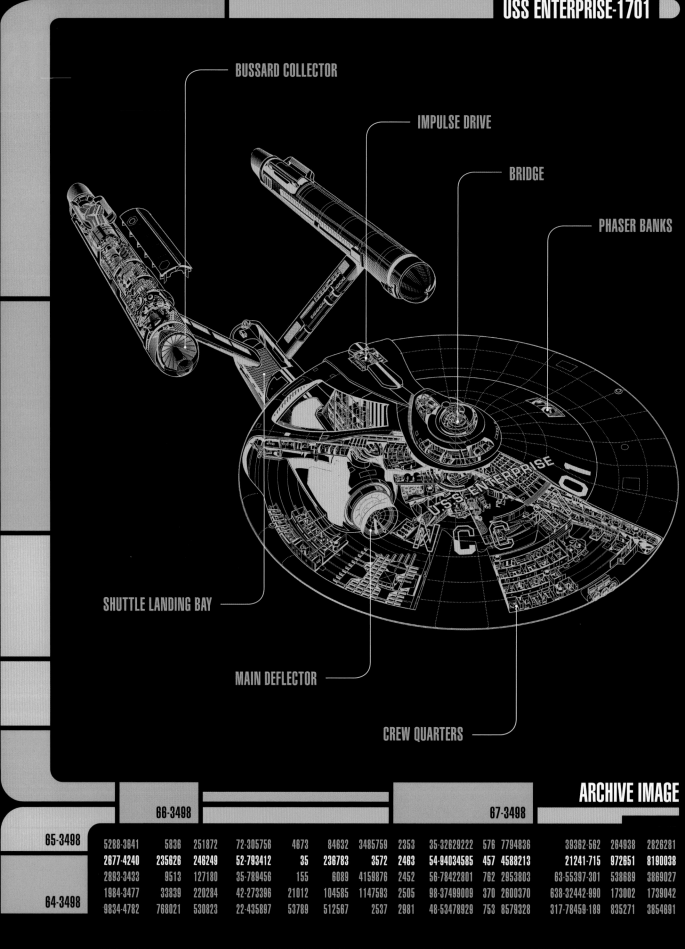

BUSSARD COLLECTOR

IMPULSE DRIVE

BRIDGE

PHASER BANKS

SHUTTLE LANDING BAY

MAIN DEFLECTOR

CREW QUARTERS

ARCHIVE IMAGE

		66-3498								67-3498				
65-3498	5288-3641	5836	251872	72-305756	4673	84632	3485759	2353	35-32629222	576	7794836	39362-562	264938	2826281
	2677-4240	235626	246249	52-793412	35	236783	3572	2463	54-94034585	457	4588213	21241-715	972651	8190038
	2893-3433	9513	127180	35-789456	155	6089	4159876	2452	56-78422801	762	2953803	63-55397-301	538689	3869027
	1984-3477	33839	220284	42-273396	21012	104585	1147593	2505	98-37499009	370	2600370	638-32442-990	173002	1739042
64-3498	9834-4782	768021	530823	22-435897	53789	512567	2537	2981	48-53478929	753	8579328	317-78459-189	835271	3854691

78478463823
4398756298340

01.10   BREAKING THE LAWS OF PHYSICS   004

INTRODUCTION
BREAKING THE LAWS OF PHYSICS

"SHE'LL LAUNCH ON TIME, SIR. AND SHE'LL BE READY."

— COMMANDER MONTGOMERY SCOTT

Space exploration has always been dangerous. Though technological advances in the 24th century have made space travel commonplace, and safer for Humanity's than in the previous four centuries, the inherent dangers of the Galaxy are no less threatening. The safety of those who travel the cosmos is dependent on the skills needed to maintain spacefaring technology and keep travelers safe from those who would do them harm. These skills are exemplified by the engineers and security officers that comprise the Starfleet operations division.

Since the days of Zefram Cochrane and Henry Archer, engineers have been crucial to the Federation's exploratory efforts. Starfleet is dependent on numerous technological advances, such as the warp drive systems that propel the fleet through the cosmos, the subspace communications network that keeps assets in the field interconnected, and the various tools and weapons employed by Starfleet personnel. A Starfleet engineer is an innovator as well as a problem solver, ingrained with the drive and inventive spirit to always be thinking of ways to improve the technology that Starfleet depends on, and ensure that it is always — as far as possible — operational. Starfleet engineers are also trained to work under pressure, as a malfunctioning warp core or an attack from a hostile craft often leaves little time to properly workshop a solution to a technological crisis.

Starfleet engineers come from a variety of backgrounds, but those who have nurtured a passion for technology and learning how things work from an early age excel more than most. Engineering cadets receive a full-bore education incorporating both the mechanical aspects of their chosen field of study as well as the applied sciences. As the maintenance of many of the devices upon which Starfleet depends is inherently hazardous if not handled with care, engineers are rigorously trained in the safe handling of equipment, such as a warp core or a transporter, and made very aware of the forces with which they deal.

Though Starfleet is primarily an exploratory and diplomatic service, the last few centuries of galactic history have more than demonstrated the need for qualified personnel trained in defense, both on the ground and at the controls of a starship's tactical systems. Starfleet security officers are the closest thing to soldiers that the Academy produces and, though Starfleet regulations encourage the defusing of any hostile situation with the barest minimum of force, security officers possess the skills and experience needed to decisively finish a fight.

YESTERDAY'S ENTERPRISE

Though **Star Trek Adventures** and this book depict events as of the game's default year of 2371 (stardates 48000-48999), Players and Gamemasters may set their campaigns in any *Star Trek* era they choose, and the Starfleet operations division has only minimal differences in its depiction in the *Enterprise* and Original Series eras. The division color was red in the previous eras as opposed to gold in *The Next Generation*, and bridge positions either had different names, such as the *Enterprise*-era "armory officer" descriptor for chief security officers; or saw their duties shifted to other bridge officers, such as the dedicated *Enterprise* and Original Series-era role of communications officer or the assignment of tactical systems control to a ship's helm officer in the Original Series Era.

A sidebar such as this will indicate if any element such as a game rule or technological advance would be unavailable in the earlier eras of play.

Though a focus on combat technique and battle strategy are key components of the security officer's skill set, Starfleet security officers fulfill other, less warfare-oriented roles in the fleet as well. Security officers are sworn law enforcement officials within Federation space and enforce the Federation's laws throughout its territory. Some security officers also pursue a career with Starfleet Intelligence, and they perform espionage and intelligence gathering missions both inside the Federation and beyond in allied and unfriendly territories. Others cross-train with the engineering department in the maintenance of a starship's integrated tactical systems.

Cadets pursuing a security career are rigorously trained in unarmed combat, marksmanship, battle strategy, and the operation and maintenance of starship weapons and defensive systems. Security cadets may supplement their training should they wish to specialize in a particular field within the security department, such as criminal investigation or counterintelligence.

Though the security department is centered primarily on defending against hostile threats, the Academy's screening processes are complex enough to weed out applicants who are simply spoiling for a fight. Security officers are trained to end hostilities, not to seek them out.

CLOSE CALL

PERSONAL LOG, STARDATE 48112.6

Well, that's the closest I've ever come to getting blown up.

I was running a group of cadet engineers on an inspection tour of the *Kiev*'s warp core, and as I'm wrapping the tour up with a Q&A session, one of the cadets raises her hand and asks me if the seal on one of the antimatter bottles was supposed to be facing that direction. Sure enough, one of the bottles' seals was misaligned and was starting to slip. Any further… well, I wouldn't be making this log entry.

Thankfully, it was in still tight enough that I could get a team down to have the thing repaired. Tomorrow, I'm going to check the sensor logs to see who I get to chew out in the morning over antideuterium handling protocols. But right now, I'm going to write a letter to the Academy Commandant and recommend that a certain Cadet First Class Mei-Xiang Chen gets her a fast-tracked commissioned post here on the *Kiev*.

PERSONAL LOG

Good morning and thanks for coming. This is a bit of a new thing for me, I must admit, so bear with me if I go off-track.

You're all here because you decided on the operations track. And you're probably wondering what an old non-com like me has to say about that. And it isn't lost on me that, barring unforeseen circumstances, I'm going to be calling every single one of you "sir" in a few years.

What I can tell you about is my experience in the two key functions of the Starfleet operations division, security and engineering. Because I've spent several years doing both. I was a tactical specialist aboard the *Rutledge* during the war with the Cardassians. Following that, I shifted to engineering, acting as senior transporter chief on the *Enterprise*… sorry if that sounds like a boast… till my, now current, position as chief of operations on Deep Space 9.

Operations division officers, in a nutshell… We get our hands dirty. We do the jobs few others can, and a lot that no one wants to. We're the guards standing brig watch or babysitting a bothersome VIP. We're the maintenance engineers fixing an ODN access line or a replicator's matter buffer. And sometimes we're the bridge tactical officer when a Borg cube warps in kilometers from our ship's bow. Or we're the chief engineer who's the only thing keeping a core breach from destroying the ship and killing the entire crew.

I won't lie, the assignments aren't always plum. The first day I walked onto DS9, it was a mess. The Cardassians did not want to let that station go. What they left that worked was substandard and everything else they went at with disruptors and hammers.

Our days are hard. Our hours are long. You will be the fallback point for every officer you serve with. We don't do our job? Command, sciences… they can't do theirs.

If I've gotten any of you close to the point of reconsidering this path, just know that you have to be prepared for the realities. But I'll say this, all the headaches and long hours going off nothing but coffee and willpower… once the job's done, it's all worth it because you made sure that your ship or your outpost was operational and safe.

That's why I'm in the operations division. And I look forward to seeing what you bring to it.

— Professor Miles O'Brien,
    Starfleet Academy, Introduction to Operations, 2376

The Operations Division supplement provides Gamemasters and Players an expanded look at the Starfleet operations division along with advice on how to apply the division's details into their campaigns. The security and engineering departments, as well as the dedicated Starfleet agencies related to them, are detailed in terms of their history within the fleet, their duties and purposes, and potential career paths for officers in each department. This book also provides new gameplay mechanics for operations division characters, such as new Focuses, Talents, Lifepath options, and career enhancements.

CHAPTER 2: OPERATIONS DIVISION

This chapter provides an expanded look at the operations division, particularly the various agencies within the fleet that provide security and engineering support to the Federation beyond the scope of a starship's crew.

Fleet Operations, the agency described in the Command Division supplement, is further detailed in terms of the subdivisions of Fleet Ops that support the missions of Starfleet's vessels and outposts, and oversee the construction efforts of those same assets. Gamemasters will be provided with advice on how to make Fleet Operations and its various subdivisions a part of their campaigns and how their Directives may affect Player Characters.

Also included in this chapter are details on the Starfleet Corps of Engineers, the agency renowned as the unparalleled masters of the engineering arts; Starfleet Intelligence, the arm of Starfleet that oversees intelligence gathering and covert operations; and Starfleet Intelligence's mysterious and morally ambiguous "cousins", Section 31. Each of these agencies are profiled in terms of their history, duties, and deployment, and Gamemasters will be provided the means to incorporate these agencies into their campaigns or center a campaign on Player Characters operating within them.

CHAPTER 3: OPERATIONS DIVISION CHARACTERS

This chapter provides Players with additional options for creating operations division characters, expanding on the character creation rules in the core rulebook. Additional Lifepath options and career enhancements are provided, as well as new Focuses and Talents for the Engineering and Security Disciplines.

CHAPTER 4: ADVANCED TECHNOLOGY

This chapter expands upon the equipment in the core rulebook and includes game statistics on advanced personal weaponry, engineering tools, and other specialized devices that fall outside the definition of standard issue equipment. Also included are advanced weapon upgrades and defensive systems for starships. Gamemasters will be advised on how to employ technology as a narrative element of their campaigns.

CHAPTER 5: USING THE OPERATIONS DIVISION

This chapter advises Gamemasters on how to best utilize and spotlight engineering and security Player Characters in their campaigns. The duties of both roles and the potential challenges they regularly face are detailed to show Gamemasters how best to incorporate them into narratives.

In addition, the sorts of mission-based storylines that typically focus on each of the operations division departments are discussed to aid Gamemasters in developing campaigns centered on Player Character operations division officers. Examples discussed include analysis of alien technology or the recovery of derelict vessels, as well as criminal investigations and security protocols for away teams.

CHAPTER 6: OPERATIONS PERSONNEL

This chapter provides full descriptions and game statistics for a variety of engineering and security focused Non-Player Characters that can be used as allies or antagonists.

CHAPTER 7: RED ALERT

This chapter provides new rules for *Star Trek Adventures* combat encounters, simplified for larger conflicts with the *Star Trek Adventures* 32mm scale miniatures. As an alternative mode of play, it provides rules for Gamemasters wishing to create tense, large scale fight scenes without slowing gameplay down.

A NASTY SURPRISE

PERSONAL LOG, STARDATE 45667

Lieutenant Commander zh'Verish really knows how to hammer a point home.

He'd set up a holodeck program that had us split up in teams of two traversing a region of rainforest in order to make it to a rendezvous point at a clearing. Lots of climbing, lots of running. Cadet Glev and I were already tiring out when the commander decided to have Borg drones beam in all over the place. Needless to say, the motivation to get to the rendezvous spiked. When we got there, he made sure we knew that an enemy won't care if you get tired or sore. Can't disagree.

PERSONAL LO

23-1

Be it known that we declare the United Federation of Planets to be our enemy.

You claim you are on a mission of peace to negotiate. We have tried to understand this word 'diplomat' but the closest we can find is 'liar'. A warrior speaks what is in their heart and makes no apology for it. To do otherwise is to dishonor us both.

23-0

You offer us gifts so we might bend our knee to you, but they insult us. We are not farmers who need to conjure food from the air. A true warrior gifts his enemy a weapon to prove he does not fear we may use it upon them. These 'replicators' and power cells are for those who work the land like slaves, all they prove is that you see us as such.

If you were a weak species, we would understand this behavior. Only an inferior race would sue for peace and offer trade and bounty for some mutual good. There are only two truths, the strong take and the weak give. You are an advanced species and a strong one, but do not behave like one which means you have no honor. We have seen how many species serve in your Federation, and we will not be claimed like those insipid slaves who you have made glad of their chains. Better we die on our feet than live in indolent luxury as a decadent people.

So I make this claim, under the five Gods of war and by the articles of honorable combat. Those scouts you sent who you call diplomats, we shall keep as our tribute, as is our right. I dare you to reclaim them and insult us further.

We expect no answer, for ours shall be the last voice in the cosmos, as it was spoken in the first times and prophesized for the final days of all things. So it is said, so it is done.

Take arms Federation. One day we will come for you.

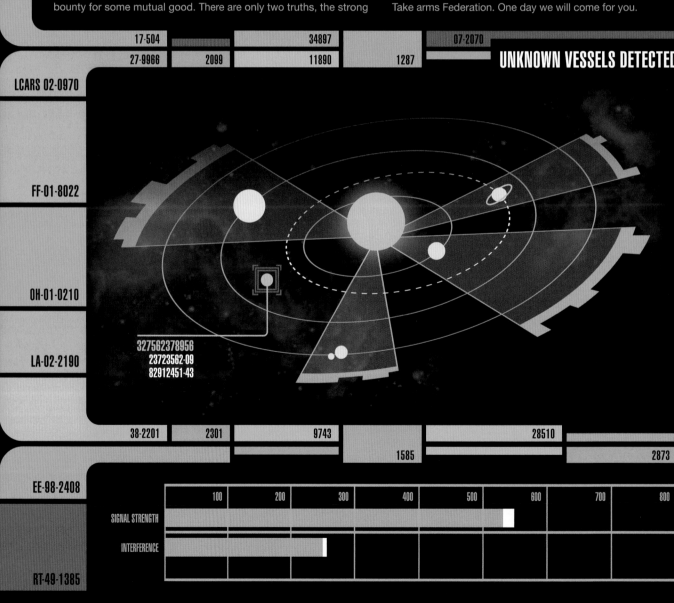

| 17-504 | | 34897 | | 07-2070 | |
| 27-9966 | 2099 | 11890 | 1287 | | |

LCARS 02-0970

UNKNOWN VESSELS DETECTED

FF-01-8022

OH-01-0210

LA-02-2190

327562378956
23723562-09
82912451-43

| 38-2201 | 2301 | 9743 | | 28510 | |
| | | 1585 | | | 2873 |

EE-98-2408

	100	200	300	400	500	600	700	800
SIGNAL STRENGTH								
INTERFERENCE								

RT-49-1385

CHAPTER 02.00

OPERATIONS DIVISION

23563462
7898245982

02.10   FLEET OPERATIONS   010

02.20   STARFLEET INTELLIGENCE   016

02.30   STARFLEET CORPS OF ENGINEERS   023

02.40   SECTION 31   029

OPERATIONS DIVISION
FLEET OPERATIONS

"CHECK WITH STARFLEET OPERATIONS. SEE IF THEIR SATELLITES PICKED UP ANY TRANSPORTER ACTIVITY THIS EVENING."

— CAPTAIN JONATHAN ARCHER

BRIEFING

Captain, we're going to expand a little on our earlier conversation regarding Fleet Operations. As you know from our earlier briefing, Fleet Ops is the agency that oversees the deployment and disposition of Starfleet personnel and resources throughout Federation space, not at all a small task given the vastness of our sphere of influence and the work needed to direct traffic amongst hundreds of vessels and installations, and countless officers and enlistees. Through meticulous record keeping, Fleet Ops maintains a detailed and regularly updated database of the actions and conditions of every sentient, starship, outpost, and piece of equipment within the fleet, as well as an archive of all mission logs, personnel reports, and scientific research. By maintaining these records, Fleet Ops has an up-to-the-minute overview of what resources are needed and where, which aids the agency in their distribution.

Fleet Operations is split into multiple subdivisions that each handle a specific aspect of Starfleet's resources; we spoke of two of those subdivisions in our earlier briefing, namely Mission Operations, which handles the planning and assignment of missions to our personnel, and Starbase Operations, which coordinates with the Starfleet Corps of Engineers to plan, construct, and maintain our starbases and outposts. We'll expand a little on those two here, as well as discuss the remainder of Fleet Ops' subdivisions, including Science Operations, who consults with Mission Operations in terms of assigning missions of scientific importance, Tactical Operations, who fulfil a similar role to Science Ops only in terms of defense and peacekeeping missions, and Shipyards Operations, who oversees Starfleet's starship construction efforts in conjunction with the Advanced Starship Design Bureau, a think tank of design engineers tasked with developing new classes of starships according to the varying needs of the fleet. The Starfleet Corps of Engineers is also technically a subdivision of Fleet Ops, but given the scope of their work, they have been afforded their own section later in this briefing.

MISSION OPERATIONS

Mission Operations, as we have previously discussed, handles the planning and assignment of Starfleet's missions to our personnel based on requests by other Starfleet divisions, the Federation Council, Federation member governments, or post commanders such as starship captains who feel a situation they have encountered requires official Starfleet intervention. Once a mission request is received by any of the aforementioned, Mission Ops employs its team of analysts to deduce the best course of action in terms of the amount and makeup of fleet personnel needed to accomplish the goal.

Mission Ops coordinates with other subdivisions within Fleet Ops depending on the type of mission, such as Science Operations and Tactical Operations.

SCIENCE OPERATIONS

Comprised of some of Starfleet's leading scientific minds, Science Operations, or Starfleet Science, fulfils much the same role as Mission Ops but geared specifically towards endeavors relating to the furtherance of scientific research, such as the charting of an uncharted region of space or a spatial phenomenon new to contemporary research. If a mission request requires scientific study, Mission Ops coordinates that request with Science Ops, so they may review the case based on Starfleet's research databases to see if the phenomenon in need of investigation could be related to anything previously discovered and which scientific disciplines would be better equipped to analyze the event in question. Starfleet Science will be explored further in a future briefing.

TACTICAL OPERATIONS

Much in the way Science Operations helps Mission Ops in dealing with missions of scientific importance, Tactical Operations assists Mission Ops in fleet deployment for missions with the potential for hostile engagement. Comprised of seasoned security officers and members of Starfleet Intelligence, Tactical Ops' team of analysts review reports of hostile engagements to predict where and how

TO: ADMIRAL HEIHACHIRO NOGURA,
STARFLEET COMMAND

FROM: REAR ADMIRAL JAMES KIRK,
FLEET OPERATIONS

Admiral, my staff has completed their review of the current state of the Sol System's patrol routes and, based on their reports, I make the following recommendations.

The inner planets' patrol fleet meets or exceeds our operational needs with one unfortunate exception, namely the *U.S.S. Ferguson*. With the catastrophic antimatter containment failure she suffered last week, I feel it goes without further explanation that the *Ferguson* should be recalled to Earth for a full overhaul and her crew be given time to heal and mourn their fallen. I know the *Ferguson*'s engineers could handle the repairs while on station and

we already have the dock crews hard at work on the fleet-wide refit to the new warp core design, but Shipyard Ops doesn't believe the *Ferguson*'s repairs will significantly overtax their engineers. I've already discussed this recommendation with Captain Axelsson and advised her that I'll greenlight the recall upon your approval. Further, I've earmarked the *U.S.S. Ansari* to replace the *Ferguson* as the patrol fleet's forward surveillance vessel during her absence.

I respectfully repeat my earlier recommendation for deploying the *U.S.S. Eisenhower* to the outer planets' patrol fleet, as I maintain that we need another cruiser on our outer line, particularly now that the *U.S.S. Shankar* has been scheduled for engine refit within the year. I'd rather not leave the outer planets shorthanded while the *Shankar* is under repairs.

At the risk of steering this report into unofficial waters and far be it from me to contribute to the delinquency of a graduating cadet, please be advised that, at the recommendation of an old country doctor of our mutual acquaintance, I've couriered over a fifth of Kentucky bourbon as a graduation gift for the newly minted Ensign Nogura. Amiko was an enormous help during her cadet internship in my office, and I'd be happy to write a letter of recommendation to any posting she has an interest in. She's done her grandfather proud, sir.

best to employ Starfleet resources in a defensive posture through analysis of non-Federation combat techniques involved and the astropolitical landscape between the Federation and their adversaries.

In addition to the tasks they perform in tandem with Mission Ops, Tactical Operations also works with other Starfleet agencies to shore up Starfleet's defensive strength, such as assisting with the development of tactical systems for starships and starbases alongside the Corps of Engineers and overseeing the supply of tactical systems to Starfleet vessels and installations in conjunction with Shipyard Operations and Starbase Operations.

SHIPYARD OPERATIONS

Shipyard Operations is the subdivision of Fleet Ops that oversees the fleet's shipbuilding facilities and the development, construction, and testing of Starfleet's array of spacecraft, from Work Bees and shuttlecraft to *Nebula*-class and *Galaxy*-class explorers. Shipyard Ops fields design commissions from both Starfleet Command and internally through the Advanced Starship Design Bureau (ASDB), a think-tank of civilian and Starfleet starship designers within Shipyard Ops, tasked with developing new starship configurations and improving upon those currently fielded through either modest redesign or full refit. Shipyard Ops is based out of Utopia Planitia Fleet Yards, Starfleet's primary shipbuilding facility that orbits Mars, but has liaison officers and ASDB auxiliary design teams based at each of the

fleet's shipyards. Dozens of starships are in various stages of construction at Utopia Planitia at any given time, a vital necessity given our expansions into new territory and the newfound uncertainty the Federation faces since the Borg incursion of 2367 and recent reports coming from Deep Space 9 regarding the Dominion.

Shipyard Ops also monitors the performance of vessels in service in conjunction with Mission Ops to determine if a ship is due for a refit, complete overhaul, or in the case of vessels with many decades of service to their credit, decommissioning and retirement. Retired ships are either disassembled for spare parts and the recycling of raw materials or, in the case of vessels with distinguished service records, restored enough to act as exhibits for the fleet's orbital museum.

STARSHIP DEVELOPMENT PROCESS

Every starship begins with one of two types of construction orders: those handed down by the Admiralty, which are immediately set into motion unless Shipyard Ops can provide a legitimate reason against doing so such as design feasibility or the availability of resources and personnel; or design proposals submitted by the ASDB, which undergo a review process enacted by Starfleet Command that evaluates these proposals in terms of feasibility, required resources, and the design's value to the fleet. ASDB proposals may be simple variants on an existing class or an entirely new class of starship altogether. Rejected design proposals may

be resubmitted should revisions be made that resolve any concerns stemming from the review process.

Whatever the source of the construction order, if approved, the ASDB begins work on fleshing out the design of the ship. Should this be a simple variant to an existing class, this process is relatively quick, as all that is needed is to modify the design to the parameters of the request. If the design is entirely new, the ASDB could spend weeks or even months on the process making sure that the ship is both adherent to the construction order and a workable design. And if the ship is a test-bed for a newly discovered technological breakthrough, the process could take even longer due to the unknown variables involved. Once completed, the design undergoes another review process overseen by Shipyard Ops and, upon their approval, the Admiralty and the joint chiefs. The vessel's name and registry number are chosen at this point; the registry numbers for class prototypes are customarily prefixed with "NX" while new vessels of existing classes are prefixed with "NCC."

If approved, Shipyard Ops reviews available drydock berths for one appropriate to the task. Most vessels are constructed at Utopia Planitia, but Starfleet maintains several smaller shipyards in both the Alpha and Beta Quadrants, most based within Sector 001, to handle overflow from Utopia Planitia

or if a specific design would be better handled by one of the auxiliary yards. Once a berth has been selected, resources are amassed, engineers are assigned, and the construction process begins. Shipyard Ops maintains a constant review of the entire process, from the building of the spaceframe and the installation of the warp core to all pre-launch diagnostics and the adornment of the vessel's registry markings.

Once construction is completed and all shipboard systems have been tested within operational parameters, Shipyard Ops performs a final inspection of the ship, deck by deck and system by system. Any concerns found during this inspection must be resolved before final approval. Once Shipyard Ops approves the design, a report is sent to Fleet Ops for final approval for a shakedown cruise, wherein a skeleton crew, either comprised of officers to be permanently assigned to the vessel or a shakedown crew of Shipyard Ops staff, perform the official launch of the ship and embark on a test cruise intended to evaluate its performance, and that of its various systems, while underway.

Any minor malfunctions during the shakedown cruise are logged and sent to Shipyard Ops and the ASDB, with whom they consult for determining solutions while underway. Major malfunctions, however, such as warp drive or life support system failure, require the shakedown crew to immediately shut the affected system down or bypass to emergency backup systems and take whatever steps needed to return to the shipyard for repairs to the faulty system. At the completion of the shakedown cruise, all the crew's logs are compiled by Shipyard Ops into a final evaluation report to Fleet Ops, who review the vessel for either approval and full deployment in the field or rejection. Shipyard Ops must address a rejection through repairs or redesign, upon which the vessel must undergo another shakedown and exceed the results of its original evaluation.

Even once deployed, a prototype's crew submits regular reports to Shipyard Ops detailing the ship's performance and any design modifications the crew has felt necessary to make while underway that either correct flaws or improve on the design. After a sufficient number of these reports indicate that the prototype is a workable design, Shipyard Ops will submit a request to Fleet Ops to have the prototype approved as a standard class of starship and authorize mass production of the class. Prototypes that have been approved for mass production will sometimes have their registry number prefix changed from "NX" to "NCC," as was done with the *U.S.S. Excelsior* when the *Excelsior*-class explorer was approved for mass production.

STARBASE OPERATIONS

As we discussed in a previous briefing, captain, Starbase Operations maintains oversight and installation of the fleet's network of starbases, the orbital and planet side installations that form the hubs of Federation presence within a region of space. Starbases provide a variety of services to civilians and Starfleet personnel such as medical care from the starbase's staff of physicians, legal intervention through the base's Judge Advocate General field office, and engineering assistance provided by an embedded Corps of Engineers team. Starbase Ops works with Fleet Ops and the Admiralty to not only select candidate sectors for starbases, often provided to a sector of space as an incentive for an alliance or Federation membership, but also to oversee construction of our starbases and collect incoming data from each base to make sure they are operational and well supplied.

The proposal and construction process for starbases is very much like that for starships, the primary differences being that Starbase Ops coordinates with any planetary governments whose area of influence encompasses the intended construction site and that the construction of the base is not directly performed by Starbase Ops but rather through the Starfleet Corps of Engineers. The structural configuration of a starbase may take a multitude of forms; it may be a planet-based complex of one or more buildings, a Class-M habitat built into a non-Class-M subplanetary body such as an asteroid or moon, or a freestanding space station that either orbits a planet or other large celestial body or is situated in deep space. Such freestanding bases use a network of reaction control thrusters for any necessary station-keeping, or to maintain and adjust their orbits.

Upon completion, starbases are brought online for a trial operational period, not unlike a starship's shakedown cruise, to ensure that the construction is sound, the base's systems are malfunction-free, and the facility can adequately house its prospective crew and civilian population as well as provide services to travelers. This trial period is monitored by a Corps of Engineers team, either the team intended for permanent assignment to the starbase or another altogether, that inspects the station top to bottom and reports their findings to Starbase Ops for final approval. Once Starbase Ops signs off on the base's trial period, the base is brought fully online and made ready for staffing and population.

FLEET OPERATIONS ORGANIZATION STRUCTURE

Fleet Ops is customarily headed by a Chief of Starfleet Operations, a Starfleet officer holding the rank of Rear Admiral at the minimum, assisted by an assistant director with the rank of captain, and the subdivisions each led by a deputy director holding the rank of either commander or captain. The Fleet Operations directorship is chosen among those officers who have excelled in their chosen career paths or overall; Fleet Operations was at one time even blessed with the leadership of Rear Admiral James T. Kirk, who accepted the post after the conclusion of his first five-year mission commanding the *U.S.S. Enterprise*.

The rank and file of Fleet Operations' staff of analysts and those of the agency's subdivisions are typically non-coms or junior officers of no greater rank than that of lieutenant commander. To qualify for duty as a Fleet Operations analyst, potential candidates must be both a qualified expert in their primary career track and an expert logistician and data analyst. A Fleet Ops analyst must be sharp-eyed, sharp-

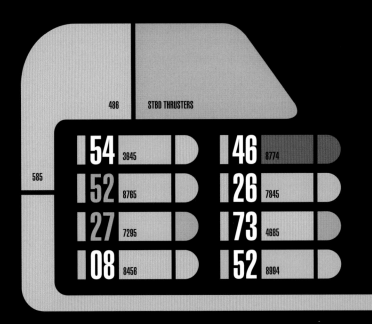

In the bygone days of Captain Archer, Fleet Operations had a far smaller sphere of influence than it does in the 24th century. With only a few dozens of ships, only a handful of which were slated for deep-space exploration, and the idea of the starbase barely an idea much less a reality, Fleet Ops functioned much in the way as it does today but at a much smaller scale, and oversaw travel to and from Earth via a network of sensor satellites that monitored incoming and outgoing starships as well as an increasing amount of transporter traffic between surface and orbit. Field offices on United Earth colonies performed this same function and would report their findings to the Fleet Operations Center in San Francisco.

As exploratory efforts expanded with the founding of the Federation and the incorporation of the space fleets of the other founders into the new UFP Starfleet, Fleet Operations' mandate evolved into the role it had during the heyday of Captain Kirk. The traffic analysis of travelers to and from Earth and the other worlds of Sector 001 was relegated to an increasingly small handful of Fleet Ops' analysts, due to the deployment of the Fleet in the Alpha and Beta Quadrants becoming the agency's primary concern and the advent of advanced sensor technology that made surveying travel through the sector a task requiring a decreasing number of personnel and resources.

minded, and able to spot trends and patterns from data originating from hundreds of reports, logs, and sensor data from throughout the Alpha and Beta Quadrants to best make recommendations for Fleet deployment.

GAME INFLUENCE

Fleet Operations is typically a ubiquitous presence with day-to-day Starfleet operations; they work behind-the-scenes to analyze reports and logs to make sure the missions assigned are accomplished and as free of adverse incident as possible, and hand out orders to flag officers in charge of a specific sector who disseminate those orders to vessels and installations assigned to their sector. Since a ship or starbase's commanding officer would normally be the only officer to deal with their sector commander for guidance and support, direct interaction between Player Characters and Fleet Operations is not unheard of but is uncommon; if Fleet Ops is doing their job correctly, interaction between them and a ship's Player Characters would only occur due to unusual circumstances.

The following are examples that Gamemasters can employ to make interaction with Fleet Ops part of their **Star Trek Adventures** campaign:

FLEET OPERATIONS IN PLAY

Fleet Ops could conceivably recall a ship to Earth or the nearest starbase to directly interact with the crew and potentially their sector commander as well. The crew might be needed for a mission that requires a level of secrecy for which only a face to face meeting would suffice. Fleet Ops could have a need to directly debrief a crew due to a mission gone wrong or a perceived discrepancy in their reports that requires clarification, or even a full investigation due to misconduct on the part of one or more crewmembers.

The crew may also use Fleet Ops as a resource. Senior staff might have need to requisition equipment upgrades specific to their present assignment from Fleet Ops. Additionally, inquiries could be made about the status of other Starfleet vessels and outposts should their present mission depend on that information, making use of their databases to analyze fleet traffic—depending on the necessary clearance. Acquiring such information could be a Task or Challenge, or incorporated into an *Obtain Information* or *Opportunity Cost* Momentum spend. Starfleet protocol deems any interactions with Fleet Operations to be handled through a posting's sector commander or done directly with authorization from the sector commander; contacting Fleet Ops without at least notifying the sector commander — technically a chain-of-command violation — should be treated as a breach of protocol and the crew should be prepared to justify such an action to their sector commander after the fact.

MISSION OPERATIONS IN PLAY

Since Mission Operations is the subdivision directly responsible for developing and assigning missions, a crew may find it necessary to consult with Mission Ops to request clarification regarding an assignment's parameters and potential hazards or request additional equipment or assistance, should the posting's personnel and equipment be substandard to the assigned task. Though mission logs from other Starfleet postings are largely free for Starfleet personnel to access, any material classified beyond a crew's security clearance would require Mission Ops to approval. Getting that clearance, or getting around it appropriately, could be a Social Conflict, with a representative of Mission Ops. Accessing the information maliciously would require a mission all of itself.

If a distress call or emergency requires a crew to postpone or abandon a mission, the crew's commanding officer is required by Starfleet regulations to notify their sector

commander, who will notify Mission Ops if they agree the diversion is necessary. Mission Ops then notes the diversion and either reassigns the mission to another posting if time is of the essence, allows the crew to return to the assignment following the diversion, or even potentially denies the crew's request to divert from their assignment. This could provide the Players with a dilemma to resolve — follow orders and allow a potential emergency to get out of hand or respond to the emergency and violate orders.

TACTICAL OPERATIONS IN PLAY

As the primary authority over Starfleet's armed engagements, Tactical Ops provides ships and starbases with any form of support needed to accomplish missions. Tactical Ops make the bulk of their databases freely available to all Starfleet postings without an approval process, but Player Characters may have their sector commander consult with the subdivision to clarify records, recommend personnel, or grant access to classified material. Tactical Ops organizes conferences, symposiums, and advanced training programs on various areas of strategy, which provide an in-game reason for Player Characters to be absent if they miss one or more game sessions.

SHIPYARD OPERATIONS

Should the Players' characters crew a starship that is less than a year off the assembly line, Shipyard Ops may make routine performance inquiries over the course of the ship's early days of deployment. Shipyard Ops may also request a crew's aid in shaking down a newly constructed vessel, either by supplementing the shakedown crew or participating in simulations intended to evaluate the new ship's systems while underway. Gamemasters may even make a shakedown cruise the opening mission for a campaign or build a mission or campaign around a Shipyard Ops shakedown rotation crew that performs shakedown cruises for starships yet to be staffed with a permanent crew; for further details on how to structure such a story, see *Chapter 5: Using the Operations Division*.

STARBASE OPERATIONS

Starbase Ops typically solely interacts with starbase crews, rarely dealing with starship crews except for unusual situations such as requesting that a ship respond to an outpost requiring assistance. Starbase Ops maintains a constant flow of information with all operational starbases and outposts, providing story points for games set aboard a starbase such as notifications of potential hazards to the base like harmful spatial phenomena or brewing hostilities in nearby space. A starbase crew may seek Starbase Ops' assistance through requisitions for personnel deployment or equipment upgrades.

OPERATIONS DIVISION
STARFLEET INTELLIGENCE

"WHAT WE WERE DOING WAS FOR THE GOOD OF THE FEDERATION, AND WE CAN'T BLAME OURSELVES IF THE OTHERS COULDN'T SEE THAT."

— REAR ADMIRAL ERIK PRESSMAN

A HIGHER STANDARD

Even an enlightened organization like Starfleet has a hand in the murky world of espionage. With the Romulan *Tal Shiar* and the Cardassian Obsidian Order manipulating the Galaxy, it would be remiss of the Federation to simply assume everyone will play nicely, especially in the intelligence arena. While other intelligence agencies resort to blackmail, coercion and even murder to learn each other's secrets and protect their own, Starfleet Intelligence is held to a higher standard as might be expected of the Federation.

Starfleet Intelligence has a simple remit: to gather intelligence on enemy operations to defend the Federation. It does not operate like a secret police force and spy on Federation citizens, does not seek out ways to leverage the officials of other species, or steal their technology. It didn't begin, however, as a benign intelligence agency and its past is full of shameful secrets: a legacy from a time of paranoia and lack of understanding that marked humanity's first steps into the stars. Even in the last few decades, Starfleet Intelligence has been responsible for several illegal and even immoral operations. When projects like the *Pegasus* came to light and were revealed by Federation personnel, Starfleet decided its intelligence executive needed a shake-up. The old guard were removed, and a more progressive executive was installed that would not compromise the ideals of the Federation, even in secret.

HISTORY

When first contact was made with the Vulcans in the 21st century, humans began to put their differences aside and work together. It had been a long time coming after years of war and bloodshed, but the people of Earth recognized they had more in common than they thought. This era initially saw an end to the old espionage agencies maintained by the various governments. Peace and harmony essentially put a lot of old spies out of work.

But it didn't last long. As the 22nd century dawned, new starships were built, and humanity began to move out into the stars. It was a frightening time and humans took their paranoia with them. While humanity had more advanced technology than it had ever possessed, there was a keen awareness of humans' status next arms to the more advanced species. Intelligence became a top priority, and many old spies were quietly recalled to service and put on as many starships and diplomatic missions as possible. There was a Starfleet Intelligence before there was really a Starfleet.

While the primary mission of these agents was information gathering their agenda was based on fear and paranoia. Behind closed doors, those who had met other alien species believed that humanity was hopelessly outmatched, and any one of these 'new friends' could potentially wipe them out in an instant. This fear informed most of intelligence service decisions. The more open and honest an alien species appeared, the more convinced were the spies that they had something to hide. Every welcoming smile seemed to be the grin of a shark; every refusal to share advanced technology was a concerted attempt to keep humanity in its place.

In the middle of the 22nd century — around the launch date of the *Enterprise* NX-01 — Starfleet Intelligence remained a shadowy organization. It stood a little apart from the rest of Starfleet and answered to different authorities. Indeed, it sometimes acted like a rogue agency and few Starfleet personnel trusted the motives of any agent they met. While these agents usually had the interests of Starfleet and humanity as their priority, this was tainted by a desire to see Earth remain secure against a myriad of imagined hostile alien schemes.

As time went on, and humanity's technology advanced, the people of Earth begun to feel a lot safer and less frightened of aliens. By the mid-23rd century the Federation was firmly established, and human technology was easily the equal of that used by the other major powers in the known Galaxy. But while Starfleet Intelligence's culture of fear had lessened, it hadn't gone away. Intelligence operations focused on those outside the Federation rather than 'any alien', partly because by this time Starfleet and its Intelligence services contained far more species than just humans. However, fear of the unknown remained and, after conflicts with the Klingons and Romulans, the Federation feared a repeat of these bloody wars. Many covert operations focused on acquiring advanced alien technology: when the Romulans developed the cloaking device, a terrified Starfleet Intelligence risked outright war with the Romulans to steal this new technology.

Even by the 24th century, the intelligence services had failed to learn from their mistakes. They had become more dedicated to the spirit of Federation edicts, but still feared they would fall behind in the never-ending race for the most advanced technology. Tired of just trying to claim the technology of others, they sought to improve on it with several new experimental devices built on discovered or stolen technology. These experiments were exceptionally dangerous, as the engineers creating devices rarely understood their principles completely. This led to many tragic accidents, most notably the *Pegasus* Incident. This attempt to create a Federation phasing cloaking device was in such direct contravention of several Romulan treaties it led to a mutiny by the Federation crew. Given the dedication to the principles of Federation drummed into each crew member, this should have come as no surprise, and it proved just how far Starfleet Intelligence had been allowed to go. The *Pegasus* itself was lost with all hands shortly after, either due to design flaws in the phasing cloak, or (as Starfleet Intelligence preferred to believe) due to an untrained attempt to shut it down. Whatever the truth, the loss of the *Pegasus* (and Starfleet Intelligence's bungled attempt at a cover up) was a wakeup call to the leaders of the Federation. It was the last straw.

The Federation instituted a purge of Starfleet Intelligence and removed almost all the "old guard", replacing them with less paranoid agents. Greater oversight was called for and those responsible for illegal missions were publicly held to account. Many agents saw this as a horrific betrayal from a naïve leadership who failed to understand the terrible dangers lurking around every corner. Some "went rogue", although many of these have quietly become deniable assets for some of the more sympathetic directors.

The new spirit of Starfleet Intelligence as a moral espionage agency has proved remarkably effective. Foreign powers have been mollified about the actions that were taken against them, or believe the Federation has pulled the teeth on one of their most effective agencies. The Obsidian Order and *Tal Shiar*, both mired in the same old school of espionage as former Starfleet agents, consider Starfleet Intelligence a spent force. They believe the Federation has once more put morals before good sense, and that such naivety will clearly lead to the destruction of the UFP.

This optimism from the enemies of the Federation has proved highly presumptuous. Starfleet Intelligence is now truly the shield of the Federation. With the focus shifted to counter espionage and defensive intelligence, they have created a protective wall of false information around the Federation. Their silent observations have granted them understanding as well as information and led to exceptional advances in diplomatic relations in the favor of the Federation. With its agents holding fast to the ideals and goals of the Federation, they are less open to corruption and collusion. While the espionage is no less dangerous, the new Starfleet Intelligence is no longer a necessary evil but a valuable part of the Federation.

ORGANIZATION

Starfleet Intelligence has a very fluid structure for a quasi-military organization. The Chief of Starfleet Intelligence and their Deputy Chief are at the top of the hierarchy. They set the general strategic objectives for the organization and represent it on the Federation council. Below them are legions of directors who manage the individual operatives. Each director has quite a broad remit to allow them to take on a wide variety of operations and make the organization highly adaptable. Many are organized into groups called "sections" to give them a specific agenda or target, although many more operate alone. This confusing organization makes it intentionally unclear about what anyone in the organization is actually doing. This might sound strange, but intelligence agents like to keep secrets, and the policy ensures that any moles don't learn too much just by being part of the agency.

At the top of Starfleet Intelligence is the office of the Chief of Starfleet Intelligence. The Chief's main job is as a figurehead and advisor. In many ways, this is a political role rather than an investigative one. The Chief acts as a special advisor to the Federation Council and represents the Intelligence services in meetings of Starfleet Command. This gives the Chief the same powers as a top-ranking admiral at Starfleet Command, and the ear of the Federation President. The power to affect policy at the highest levels of the Federation makes some people very nervous. The Chief is often extremely busy, being called at a moment's notice to advise the President on the details of diplomatic situations, so the Deputy Chief is left to run the organization on a day to day basis. In fact, most of the work of running Starfleet Intelligence is done by the Deputy Chief, giving an insight into the "big picture" that will be required when moving up to Chief. The Deputy Chief oversees the various directors and passes on the strategic operations and policy that the directors need to implement.

As the office of the Chief is all about the "big picture", the directors are given leeway to work out operational details. They will be told where to focus their efforts, but how they go about their work is up to them. They decide what actual missions need to take place to achieve the objectives set down by the Office of the Chief. They assign agents and create mission plans with individual agents. While many directors work alone, most are assigned a section which gives them an area where they need to focus their efforts. It is rare for a director to be reassigned between sections, as it can take years to truly understand the intricacies of each espionage arena.

Working for the directors are the rank and file agents, who operate in one of two ways: investigative agents and covert agents. Much as might be expected, covert agents perform undercover work and carry out spy missions within Federation space and outside it. Investigative agents act as detectives in matters of domestic espionage and where Starfleet Intelligence needs to "put a face" on things. Unsurprisingly, most agents are covert. In fact, unless a recruit proves to have an aptitude for investigative work, almost all begin their career as covert agents for a simple reason: spies in rival intelligence agencies take note of anyone who claims to be Starfleet Intelligence, so both the *Tal Shiar* and Obsidian Order maintain lists of all investigative agents at Starfleet Intelligence! It is usually only when a covert agent's cover is blown, or they decide to retire from field work, that an agent moves to the investigative department. Investigative work also gives an agent a feel for working within the politics of Starfleet and the Federation, and so most directors are chosen from the pool of investigative agents. For this reason,

there are very few investigative agents, as most become directors once an opening is available.

Covert agents perform all the tasks you'd expect of a spy. They infiltrate other organizations and seek out intelligence on the operations run by enemy powers. They report to their director, sometimes through a handler (who may be an investigative or another covert agent), and never reveal their affiliation to anyone. To do their job, each covert agent usually has a cover, and spend a good deal of time maintaining this cover. Starfleet Intelligence prefers to play the long game and trains its agents not to risk their cover for the sake of intelligence. One juicy bit of information at the cost of a blown cover is usually not worth as much as all that might be learned by remaining hidden. Of course, this doesn't apply when there are lives on the line.

While most take on civilian roles, many covert operatives maintain a cover as Starfleet crew and even officers. Sometimes this is for a specific mission, at other times it is just to place agents where they might be required later. For instance, an agent might be placed on a ship patrolling near the Badlands, so they can take on anti-Maquis missions if a need arises. To alleviate the paranoia of starship captains, all covert agents on Federation starships are required to reveal their identity to their captains, but not their mission. Captains

with first officers ideally only in an emergency, and to no one else. In some cases, this arrangement works very well. Agents function as crew members, but work with their captains to maintain cover; in return they keep Captains up to date on matters of intelligence. Covert agents have access to vast amounts of useful information and can become valuable secret advisors. However, more often than not captains always wonder what the intelligence agents are reporting about their ships and come to resent the fact there are people under their command who are not entirely responsible to them.

NOTEWORTHY SECTIONS

There are many divisions and sub-divisions called sections run by various directors. Many are run jointly by several directors, others by just one: it depends on the scale and scope of the section in question, and these sections are very fluid. They can be reassigned and reordered very quickly, although some have stood as they are for decades or even centuries. Many have specific titles, others are known by little more than a code or a number (such as the rumored "Section 31") to keep their portfolio a secret. The directors either work together in a section or pursue operations without a specific agenda on their own. All of them keep the office of the Chief of Starfleet intelligence informed of their plans and progress. While there are many sections, a few of the more well-known are worth detailing further:

FOREIGN AFFAIRS

As might be imagined, there are large sections dedicated to keeping an eye on the operations of each of the major powers in the Galaxy. The Section for Klingon Affairs has slowly shifted from being one of the largest departments to now operating mostly under the jurisdiction of the Section for Federation Security. Operative assigned to the Romulan or Cardassian sections are usually among the best and brightest, given the espionage skills of their opponents. In fact, many consider a posting there to be the ultimate test of an agent.

Two new sections have recently been created. Given their advanced technology and interest in Earth, the first of these is dedicated to the Borg. The other new section is dedicated to the Dominion, and intelligence operations by this section have proved vital as the Dominion continues to get involved in the Alpha Quadrant.

ARCHIVES

Starfleet Intelligence keeps several small archives that contain records of their operations and secrets in the most secure areas in the Federation. These secrets are too important to be kept in one place but keeping them in a lot of different places offers a higher chance of discovery. Many of the Intelligence archives are kept in standard Federation archives, but in secret parts few people know about. In this way Intelligence agents hide their secrets in plain sight, keep them in the right type of facility and can access them while appearing to visit a public archive.

EXPERIMENTAL TECHNOLOGY

This section has had its problems in the past. Responsible for the disastrous *Pegasus* mission, Experimental Technolo has seen a major shake-up over the last few years. It is still a bastion for the few agents who remain deeply concerned that the Federation may be losing a galactic arms race. The section has much less autonomy than it once had, and fewer agents, but it is prepared to go further than most in the pursuit of advanced technology to keep the Federation ahead of its rivals.

DOMESTIC SECURITY

This is the most controversial section in Starfleet Intelligenc and one they like to avoid mentioning whenever possible. It was one of the earliest divisions to be set up, originally designed to spy on the Vulcans as humanity formed a new alliance. Since then it has broadened its mission to spy on — "monitor" — Federation member worlds, and they are supposed to keep an eye on potential instabilities within the Federation. Using gathered intelligence, diplomats have bee forewarned of intricacies in particular situations, and this ha allowed them to smooth the waters between members befo anything went bad. Many argue that the work of Domestic Security is what keeps the Federation together, detractors remain concerned it could easily become a secret police force, or a system to keep minor species in line with the needs of major species like Humans and Vulcans.

OPERATIONS

Starfleet Intelligence carries out a very wide range of missions and operations. It is up to the directors to conceiv and implement each operation to meet the agenda set by the Office of the Chief. The directors usually only receive strategic commands, rather than detailed missions. One might be told that there are concerns that the Romulans ha a spy on a starbase: it will be up to the director to decide th best way to go about finding any spy. Maybe the director already has an agent in place on the base, maybe he knows a Romulan contact he can lean on, perhaps he'll send a strike force to a data vault, or maybe he'll decide to leave a trail of disinformation to uncover the mole.

While directors have a wide range of options in deciding mission parameters, since the *Pegasus* incident there are limits. Other espionage organizations will stoop to almost any methods to get what they want: blackmail, bribery, corruptio theft and even murder. Starfleet Intelligence works without performing such activities unless there is a direct threat to the lives of Federation citizens. It is primarily a counter-intelligenc organization and works to protect the Federation rather than steal enemy technology, or sow dissent among the opposing powers. If you leave the Federation alone, you have little to fear from Starfleet Intelligence.

Even with a more enlightened policy, Starfleet Intelligence still has a lot of operations running across the galaxy. The following are some of the most common mission types run by Starfleet Intelligence. There are innumerable ways to approach any problem, of course, and most directors have their own, different views about the best course of action for a particular goal.

INFILTRATION

The most common operation for Starfleet Intelligence is infiltrating the enemies of the Federation. Most operatives spend their time in deep cover, watching and listening to the activities of a target group, usually a non-Federation species. There are also plenty of criminal, political or terrorist groups that need to be carefully observed. These operations are vital to taking these groups down. With more oversight, Starfleet Intelligence needs clear evidence that action needs to be taken against any particular group. After all, some innocent agitator groups might get labelled as "terrorist organizations" in a less enlightened society. Starfleet Intelligence needs to ensure it allows citizens the right to protest, but without endangering the safety of the Federation. This means that clear and detailed evidence is important, not only to ensure a group can be properly dealt with but also to ensure the operation is legal. Such infiltration missions might be short or very long term, but they are designed to make sure that when Starfleet Intelligence makes a move, it can clear everything up in one fell swoop.

When it comes to terrorist groups like the Maquis, accurate intelligence is vital. These groups often operate as individual cells, and such cells are easily replaced. Infiltrators need to get deeper into the organization to make sure that they are taking down its central command. In the case of the Maquis, the political waters are a lot murkier. Starfleet Intelligence's central task is the protection of the Federation and its citizens, but the Maquis are dedicated to fighting the Cardassians and so pose little threat to the Federation. They are also Federation citizens and therefore in need of protection when the Cardassians get heavy handed. However, allowing the Maquis to act unchecked damages Cardassian-Federation relations and might lead to war, something that is clearly a threat to Federation security. Starfleet intelligence often plays both sides to maintain what remains of the fragile peace. Operatives have taken down hardline Maquis cells when they were ready to accept civilian casualties or attack facilities that would force a war. They have saved Cardassians whose deaths would have brought a heavy-handed Cardassian response and led supply columns between Cardassian blockades to make sure colonists get the food and supplies they need. The situation is a minefield of violence and cold war politics, and operatives working on the Maquis issue risk their lives on a daily basis.

When it comes to foreign powers, Starfleet Intelligence takes a long-term approach. Their agents operate without much support deep in the territory of other powers. They must be careful as they will usually be executed if their cover is blown. Their goal is to get as close as they can to the leadership, so they can report any potential threat to the Federation, working themselves slowly and carefully into the trust of those in power, and only risking their cover in the direst of circumstances. This is often made more difficult when some powers will use disinformation to convince an agent there is a credible threat to the Federation, so they blow their own cover to warn their superiors. Understanding and verifying any data an agent learns is a vital skill as their l life may depend it.

VERIFYING INTELLIGENCE

It is very rare for intelligence information to be clear and precise. Agents do their best to get as much detail as they can and ensure its accuracy before they pass data on to the Federation, but that is not often very easy to do. For instance, if an attaché discovers the Cardassians are building a weapons platform on Gellin 6, there is little they can do to verify this is the case without going to Gellin 6. In such cases a team needs to visit a target area and ascertain the truth of what the Cardassians are doing. These missions are often very dangerous as they are usually in enemy territory. Just being caught might lead to arrest and even execution. Given the original agent needs to maintain their cover, a different team needs to be sent on the verification mission. ThThese teams can be covert agents but are usually investigative agents. Starfleet Intelligence often seconds Starfleet personnel to carry out this kind of mission, especially if they are on a ship near the right area.

MANAGING DEFECTIONS

Outside the Federation there are many oppressive regimes. Their governments tell their citizens that what they hear about the utopian Federation is just propaganda. Not everyone believes the propaganda, and some may decide they want to make a new life in the Federation. While the Federation doesn't have the resources to manage escapes for everyone, occasionally a high-ranking member of a foreign regime wants to defect. In such cases defector may bring information that makes it worthwhile to aid their escape. The more highly placed a defector, the more ardently their regime will work to ensure they can never leave. Defection operations can be among the most dangerous undertaken by an agent because they must blow their own cover to the defector to facilitate the plan. Some loyal members of a regime will intimate a wish to defect to see if it provokes an approach. It can be a very effective way to uncover spies, so an agent needs to be very careful.

The Romulans are especially adept at this tactic and used the lure of a Senator's support for Romulan/Vulcan reunification to bring Ambassador Spock to Romulus. He was then manipulated with plans for a mass defection of Romulans looking to 'return' to Vulcan, although in truth it was all a plot to send an invasion force to Vulcan! The plan was only just foiled in time, but the fact they outmaneuvered Spock proved they are not to be underestimated.

ACQUIRING ADVANCED TECHNOLOGY

While the failures of the *Pegasus* mission remain very fresh in the memory, Starfleet Intelligence does still have a remit to acquire technology. Their plans in this area are strictly monitored and no action in breach of any treaty is authorized. While many would like to get their hands on a cloaking device again, they concern themselves more with potential uses and users of illegal technology. There are several weapon types that are deemed too horrifying to use, and have been made illegal under galactic law, such as Varon-T disruptors and thalaron radiation generators. Not all governments outside the Federation are happy to play by the rules so Starfleet Intelligence keeps a close eye on new, emerging technologies to try and ascertain if they are based on any banned technological advances.

It is also important to know more about what weapons other powers are developing so the Federation can develop appropriate defenses. In a bid to sidestep some of the new regulations, agents are sometimes sent to find out about new technology but not to try and duplicate it. What Starfleet Intelligence wants is detail on the weaknesses and vulnerabilities of any new technology rather than plans or prototypes.

STARFLEET INTELLIGENCE IN PLAY

Given how secretive Starfleet Intelligence is, it can be tricky to introduce its plots into a standard campaign. However, it is possible for individual Player Characters to be part of Starfleet Intelligence and for the whole player character group to be assigned missions on behalf of Starfleet Intelligence.

JOINING STARFLEET INTELLIGENCE

Most operatives of Starfleet Intelligence are not part of Starfleet. Covert agents are usually placed in deep cover for many years. While their lives are in constant danger, they don't have many adventures unless things go badly wrong. Investigative officers are more involved in Starfleet, but usually work inside the Federation assisting the diplomatic corps. The best option for a player character who is part of Starfleet Intelligence is for them to be a covert agent who maintains their cover as a Starfleet Officer (or crewman) on a working starship.

There isn't a career path in terms of character generation that needs to be followed. Starfleet Intelligence recruits people who show an aptitude for the sort of skills they need and have the right personality for this sort of work. Such people are quite rare and so they are recruited wherever they are found. Luckily, the most important traits — a love of the Federation and a resolute duty to protect it — are common among Starfleet personnel.

If a player wants their character to be part of Starfleet Intelligence, it is really up to the Gamemaster to allow it. They should have good Control and Insight (and a good Daring never hurts). Their Security Discipline will be the most useful, but a diverse range of Disciplines is often just as useful. They should also have a good range of espionage related Focuses, such as Composure, Infiltration and Persuasion. Ultimately, it is up to the Gamemaster to look at the character's skills and decide if they have the "right stuff". To make this decision easier we've included a new Career Event for the Lifepath that helps to ensure a character has what's needed.

If a character fits the bill and the Gamemaster allows it, they are a member of Starfleet Intelligence. They will have been assigned a mission to make reports on the area their ship has been assigned to and may be given certain clandestine missions as well. Their ship's Captain (which may not be the Player character agent) will know their status, which might make things easier or harder. Sometimes they will be given missions they need help with, and at that point it will be up to them to decide if they need to bring in the other Player Characters...

NEW CAREER EVENT

RECRUITED TO STARFLEET INTELLIGENCE

On a quiet day while you were on shore leave, you were approached by a member of Starfleet Intelligence and offered a position as a covert agent. It seems they had been watching you for some time and decided you had the right skills and attitude they required. You were assigned a small mission as a test, and if you passed they promised to take you on as an agent, but one that maintained your Starfleet career.

- Did you pass the test and accept their offer?

- What did you have to do on the mission? Did you have to make any moral choices?

- If you did decide to join, what convinced you? Was it the excitement, the desire to learn more secrets, or just because you were frightened of what might happen if you refused?

Attribute: The character keeping their cool undercover and improvising plans increases their Daring by 1.

Discipline: To perform the mission the character needed to employ all their stealth and quick thinking, increasing their Security by 1.

Focus: Depending on the mission the character might have learned covert skills. Examples include: Composure, Infiltration or Persuasion.

agents in the dark as they have found operatives are far more effective when they know all the facts. Even if the whole truth is a little embarrassing for the Federation, it also allows an agent to improvise and adapt their plans with far more skill and precision. Starfleet Intelligence has a lot less "ego" than its contemporaries and prepares its agents better than any other agency. However, where there is a threat of capture some details may be on a "need to know" basis.

Most of missions involve verifying intelligence. When Starfleet Intelligence needs someone to look at a particular area, a nearby starship may be tasked to do so. If a scan of the area isn't enough to verify the data, a team may have to be sent in. This is quite common as most secret installations have some sort of cloaking field or jamming system. The team sometimes only needs to get close enough to verify the existence of an installation, but usually will need to make sure it serves the expected purpose. If an operative discovers the Romulans have a weapon production facility near a Federation colony just seeing there is a Romulan base, there is not enough. Confirm it makes weapons and not just self-sealing stem bolts is required, otherwise any accusations will lead to diplomatic incidents. It is not uncommon for Romulans and others to build "secret", but innocent, installations to provoke such accusations. Wrong accusations can be turned to diplomatic advantage when the Federation is forced to apologize.

While some intelligence verification missions can be straight forward, most are not. They often involve entering hostile areas, and sometimes making illegal landings on sovereign territory. When it comes to illegal landings some diplomacy may also be required. The starship will need to have a reason to enter the area in the first place, and usually a diplomatic mission provides a decent cover. In such cases a player character group might be divided between the two parts of the mission. One group makes the landing to carry out the mission while the others use diplomatic tricks to keep enemy attention on them and give the covert group as much time as possible.

There are a host of other missions to which a Starfleet crew might be seconded. As well as intelligence verification, it is common for them to help get defectors away from hostile regimes, rescue Federation citizens being used for blackmail (such as families of officers) or track down enemy agents that have been discovered in Federation space.

While it is difficult for Starfleet Intelligence to perform more overt missions, they do come up. As long as an enemy regime will be unable to admit their part in the mission (such as the establishment of an illegal installation) Starfleet Intelligence can be open in its work. For such missions borrowing a Starfleet vessel is the best option. Starfleet Intelligence is the shield of the Federation, but when it needs a sword as well it turns to Starfleet. That is where the Player Characters come in.

CO-OPTING THE PLAYER CHARACTERS

While it is possible to play an intelligence officer as part of a player group, it is difficult. Any missions they work on for Starfleet Intelligence will be classified and not for anyone outside the intelligence service to know about. This is fine if you are running a game for a solo player, or the group are all intelligence operatives. In a mixed group everyone else will either be left out of the adventure or not know what is really going on.

Luckily, Starfleet Intelligence does a lot of outsourcing. With most of its agents working on deep cover missions or spread out across the Galaxy, the intelligence service relies a lot on Starfleet itself. It is very common to send a group of Starfleet officers on a mission under the command of Starfleet Intelligence. In many cases an Investigative agent may be sent with the team to run the mission or act as a liaison.

While such missions are highly classified, the entire player character group might be chosen for such a mission and therefore be aware of the same brief. They will be under strict orders not to share any details of the mission (even the fact the mission exists) with anyone else, but they can talk freely among themselves. Unlike the *Tal Shiar* or the Obsidian Order, Starfleet Intelligence does not believe in keeping its

OPERATIONS DIVISION
STARFLEET CORPS OF ENGINEERS

"...I'M WILLING TO BET THAT YOU'VE BROUGHT ONE OF THOSE FAMED STARFLEET ENGINEERS WHO CAN TURN ROCKS INTO REPLICATORS."

— KEEVAN

MIRACLE WORKERS

Starfleet captains don't have to be reminded of the immense value of Starfleet Corps of Engineers (SCE) to the Federation. Pretty much everything in Starfleet that isn't a spacecraft was designed and built by the SCE, and we depend immensely on them to keep the Fleet operational and on the cutting edge of technological development, as well as deploying their engineers to handle technological dilemmas beyond the capabilities of a starship's or starbase's engineering department.

An officer will deal with the Corps at various occasions during a command tour, receiving their assistance or helping them, so this briefing will detail their history, organization, and methodologies.

ORGANIZATION AND DEPLOYMENT

The Corps of Engineers' leadership is housed at Starfleet Headquarters on Earth and consists of a Command Liaison (holding at least captain's rank) and several subordinate commander-level deputy directors. These deputies oversee a sector of space; a qualified expert in a field of engineering discipline; or liaisons to other Starfleet agencies such as Starbase Operations or Shipboard Operations. Since SCE is a subdivision of Fleet Operations, the director of Starfleet Engineering is directly subordinate to the Chief of Starfleet Operations in the overall chain of command.

Corps personnel are deployed throughout Federation space as teams, either mobile and assigned to a dedicated starship, or embedded long-term at a starbase or outpost. Several teams are often combined as larger crews needed for big projects such as the construction of outposts or civil engineering projects commissioned by a Federation member or ally. The number of personnel assigned to each team varies according to need and availability. Mobile teams may

number as few as six and as many as ten, starbase teams twice or three times that, while construction crews for larger projects are often multiple teams numbering a hundred or more. Though shipbuilding efforts are the province of Shipyard Operations, several SCE personnel serve aboard Starfleet's shipyards as consulting subject matter experts, and as members of the Advanced Starship Design Bureau group assigned to each shipyard. The yard's Engineering Corps liaison officer acts as their direct superior.

The SCE receives most of its project assignments in the form of orders from Fleet Operations, who receive multitudes of requests from Starfleet Command, the Federation Council, and the sovereign governments of Federation members and allies. Project assignments are evaluated by the director of Starfleet Engineering, who determines what skill sets are needed; what Starfleet Engineering teams would be suitable and within travel range; the challenges inherent in the project; and prospective completion time. If the director of Starfleet Engineering signs off on a request, a team deploys to the site and orders requisitions of any equipment and materials needed. Should a project take an inordinate amount of time, the director may choose to rotate the project among multiple teams to limit fatigue or other personnel factors that would not only affect the quality of the project but potentially place the assigned personnel at risk.

PROJECT PROFILES

Starfleet Engineering missions can encompass all sorts of engineering challenges far beyond what this briefing could possibly detail. However, we will discuss some of the SCE's more frequent mission profiles and what is involved in performing these duties.

STARBASE AND OUTPOST CONSTRUCTION AND REPAIR
Much like Shipyard Operations oversee Starfleet shipbuilding, the SCE is responsible for the construction of starbases. Every starbase begins as a request from Fleet

After nearly a year, we're down to the last cubic kilometer of rock. Once we have this drilled out, the Doctors Marcus' cave of… whatever it is will be ready for them to take charge. And I can't say it'll be too soon.

Don't get me wrong. The Corps has sent me and the guys to more than a few hellholes to patch things up or get something built, and this job's just another day at the office. It's this need-to-know stuff that bothers me. Tunneling out a dead planetoid for some top-secret science experiment that we can't be told even the slightest detail and that had us reassigned here and off the aqueduct project on Theta Phi IV, a job that stood to help a lot of people… it's the height of annoyance to not have some semblance of what this whole thing's about. I'd like to think this cave we're digging isn't just a weird vacation home or something.

Mental note: make a stop back to Theta Phi IV to see how that job panned out since Commander th'Nelev's team took over. The archaic automation software on those waterflow regulators was a programmer's nightmare and I'd like to see if his team figured it out.

There's also Doctor Marcus Junior. David. The bulk of the Project Genesis staff's been very accommodating to me and the team, with that one key exception. I don't know what his beef with Starfleet is, but it thankfully won't be my problem much longer since we're maybe a few weeks from calling this job done and dusted. I've had about as many of his smelling-onions glares and 'evil military industrial complex' speeches to last me the decade.

Mental note: reprogram David's sonic shower to blast 21st-century Earth thrash metal at full volume before we leave for redeployment.

In any case, that one or two thorns in my side notwithstanding, it's been an interesting and challenging year, but I'll be glad to have this giant cave of classified something or other finished, and I hope our next job is somewhere that doesn't require ten-hour shifts in EV suits."

— Commander Simone Giertz, Commanding Officer,
  Starfleet Corps of Engineers Team 17-Bravo

PERSONAL LOG

Operations, who determine the need for a starbase based on multiple factors: the necessity of a permanent Starfleet presence within a sector of Federation or allied space; a response to a request from a higher body of authority such as Starfleet Command or the Federation Council; or as political incentive for current or potential Federation allies. Once the request is approved following a review process by senior SCE staff, the Corps surveys the sector for a suitable construction site and assigns a starbase construction crew. This comprises multiple engineering teams, the exact number depending on the intended base size and the likely construction difficulty.

Starbases go through much the same construction and inspection processes as starships. Starbases have classes just like starships, and this enables the Corps to build from any number of preexisting configurations with minimal preparatory design time, making modifications as needed to tailor the class to the individual mission parameters and to answer any concerns posed by the base's surroundings on a spatial, environmental, or political level. Once construction is complete, the Corps performs a lengthy and rigorous inspection process, wherein the construction crew is advised of any faults in their work that require correction. Once all concerns are addressed, or in the absence of any faults, the inspectors sign off the base which is brought online and made ready for staff assignments and population. Unless

deployment elsewhere is deemed necessary, the engineering construction team is usually embedded with the base's staff for a long period.

INVESTIGATION OF ALIEN TECHNOLOGIES

The Corps of Engineers often receives requests for aid from throughout the Federation whenever personnel encounter technology of unfamiliar origin in the field, whether the item in question originates from a culture familiar to the Federation, a newly encountered one, or an ancient civilization long dead. Filing a request of this nature is not mandatory as the personnel encountering the technology may have the skills to investigate the item, but a Corps team can be called in if additional expertise is needed. The SCE has strict protocols for handling unfamiliar technologies to ensure that examination or activation of any unknown devices poses no risk to life.

DISASTER RELIEF

Should a Federation world or allied planet suffer any cataclysmic event that causes damaging effects to vital portions of its infrastructure (such as wide-scale property damage or loss of basic resources), an SCE team may be assigned to perform necessary repairs to restore the affected area. These requests for aid usually come from Fleet Operations, whose monitoring of Federation space would alert them to any such situation. Starfleet also responds to requests for disaster assistance from allies or frontier worlds that fall outside Fleet Ops' purview. Starfleet considers any sort of disaster-relief request a high priority and will often send at least one starship to lend medical aid and to supplement the work of on-site SCE personnel. Multiple SCE teams may be dispatched to handle such a situation depending on the scale and severity of a disaster.

ASSISTANCE WITH CIVILIAN PROJECTS

Civilian organizations within the Federation such as planetary governments, scientific research institutes, or industrial firms may petition the Federation Council for assistance with large-scale research or construction projects. Should the Council deem the potential benefits of such a proposal worthwhile, the Council will send a deployment order to Fleet Operations, which then issues assignments regarding the project to its various subdivisions, including the Corps of Engineers if the project requires engineering assistance. Personnel will thus be deployed to provide design and construction assistance for the project as well as any additional needed materials. SCE command personnel on-site work with the civilian project management to oversee construction, but they also submit regular project reports to Fleet Operation. The project may be a collaborative effort, but Starfleet has a vested interest due to resources committed. It needs to be informed of any unforeseen circumstances that affect the project or pose a risk to the SCE personnel involved.

SALVAGE

The Corps is often called on for salvage operations for derelict starships or inoperative outposts. This can include determining if a damaged craft or outpost can be restored to operational capacity and, if the damage was caused by something unknown, to determine what caused the ship or station to be left in such a state. Salvaging a damaged starship or outpost can be a dangerous task due to such hazards as radiation leaks, hull breaches, and environmental system failure. Corps engineers maintain safety protocols for salvaging derelicts, which are nearly identical to those in place for investigating alien technologies.

DISTRESS CALL RESPONSE

Starships and starbases, belonging to Starfleet or others, may find themselves dealing with systems malfunctions that places the ship or facility and its personnel at great risk: a failure of life support or antimatter containment is truly threatening. An SCE team within proximity may be called on to respond to such an emergency should the engineering crew detachment be unable to resolve the situation themselves. Once aboard, the SCE works with the local engineering team and resolves the issue or, in cases of severe damage or irreparable malfunctions, recommends that the ship or facility is no longer safe. The SCE team then assist an evacuation. If a fatal design flaw is discovered to have caused the emergency, the SCE deputy director in charge of the team's area of operations will send the team's findings to other Starfleet agencies so that similar emergencies elsewhere can be prevented.

SCE SAFETY REGULATIONS

INVESTIGATION OF TECHNOLOGICAL ELEMENTS OF INDETERMINATE ORIGIN

- Full diagnostics are to be performed on all equipment and transport to be used by the investigation team prior to arrival at the investigation site to ensure against harmful data intrusions or anything that would endanger sentients.

- A Starfleet medical officer should be on site for the duration of the investigation to deal with any injuries to sentients occurring during the investigation.

- Full sensor scans of the item from a remote distance are to be performed upon commencement of investigation to determine the item's potential of risk to sentient life.

- All applicable safety measures must be employed before personnel come into contact with the item.

- Any physical manipulation of the item or introduction of power or data to the item must be preceded by tricorder scans to verify that any such action will not prove harmful to personnel present.

- If the item is considered a danger to life that safety measures cannot contain, personnel must notify superiors of the hazard, take steps to evacuate any sentient beings within the potential area of effect, and redirect the investigation towards the removal of the item.

CULTURAL OBSERVATION SUPPORT

The SCE routinely provides engineering aid to Starfleet or civilian cultural observation teams surveying neighboring civilizations who are unaware of other sentient life. They assist with using hidden observation posts, holographic isolation suits, or assimilating within a culture while disguised as a native with reconstructive surgery. Maintaining the equipment (and therefore the illusion that aliens are not among a culture under observation) is imperative per the Prime Directive, the SCE's skills are greatly in need for these missions, particularly if the Federation determines that a culture needs a diplomatic first contact. This presumes the observed culture develops native warp-drive technology, which increases the likelihood of the culture discovering the existence of other sentient life on their own. The SCE also assists with first contact missions by evaluating a culture's technological advancements for the purposes of record keeping and to ensure that, should the culture ever petition for Federation membership, the species adheres to Federation law in terms of not developing legally forbidden technologies, such as biogenic weapons or cloaking technology.

TERRAFORMING SUPPORT

Terraform Command, the civilian Federation agency that manages terraforming efforts throughout the Federation, routinely consults with the SCE to ensure that prospective worlds have everything required for a successful terraform. Federation and allied terraforming projects are often aided by the Corps of Engineers during the process, by means such as installation and repair of environmental habitats, water and atmospheric filtration systems, and sensor arrays that monitor the status of newly introduced biospheres. As terraforming projects can take decades to complete, multiple SCE interventions may be necessary over the project's lifetime.

YESTERDAY'S ENTERPRISE

The Corps of Engineers is less evident in the *Enterprise* and Original Series time periods, owing both to the SCE's infancy and Starfleet's favoring peacekeeping and exploration with resources. In the *Enterprise* era the SCE doesn't even exist prior to the late 2150s (when the first Earth starbase is constructed following the events depicted in *Star Trek: Enterprise*). It numbers only a few hundred people, mostly assigned to Earth and other colonized worlds and outposts within Sector 001. A campaign set in this period would be unlikely to encounter a Corps presence unless the crew were on or near Earth, where SCE personnel of the time were often working on civil engineering projects, designing and building outposts, or consulting with Shipyard Ops and the Advanced Starship Design Bureau.

With the expansion of the Federation into the Original Series, the Corps' numbers grew to the point that the first field teams, at that time including civilian engineers as well as Starfleet personnel, were introduced and embedded aboard starships. This allowed

Starfleet Engineering to lend their expertise to the remainder of the Federation, and there is more likelihood that Player Characters will encounter the SCE in much the same way as they would in *The Next Generation*. SCE teams of the Original Series era were often underequipped and had as many civilians as Starfleet engineers; the professional discipline usually associated with Starfleet personnel may be lacking or entirely absent. Some SCE engineers of this period may be embittered by the fact that Starfleet expects them to perform their duties with scant resources compared to those allotted to exploratory starship crews. This could provide a source of drama, such as a disagreement over methodology or protocol.

TO: COMMANDER ELIZABETH SHELBY, RECOVERY TASK FORCE

FROM: COMMANDER DONALD HAWKINS, S.C.E. TEAM 83-ECHO, EMBEDDED ABOARD U.S.S. WOZNIAK

Our work is done, Commander. And I hope I never have to do anything like this again.

My team has completed the survey of the wreckage of the ships we lost to the Borg. The medical team here has collected and identified all bodily remains and notified next of kin. We've still dozens we're unable to locate per the crew manifests; I'm afraid we have no choice to list them as missing and presumed deceased. If they were assimilated en route to Earth, chances are they met the same fate as the cube, rest their souls.

Of the forty ships comprising Admiral Hansen's armada, only the U.S.S. Ahwahnee is of sufficient condition for repair and return to service, and even then, the damage sustained in the battle is going to require a lot of work. The EPS conduit network was overloaded to the point that the whole system is cooked; the plasma charges resulting from that caused many of the on-board fatalities. At least three decks were vented to vacuum s[o] there's a lot of explosive decompression damage to address, and the starboard ventral nacelle will have to be completely replaced. I've appended to this report the laundry list of repair[s] Shipyard Ops will need to do to get her space worthy again. I estimate it'll take months, but it can be done.

As for the remaining vessels… Elizabeth, there's no other wa[y] to put it. None of what's left of these ships will ever fly again. Whether we're talking spaceframe, systems, propulsion… all[l] these ships would take far longer to repair than just replace. I recommend that Shipyard Ops send out a salvage crew and that Fleet Ops declares all thirty-nine officially lost in the line of duty. The Wozniak will stick around till they arrive to make sure no profiteers try grave robbing.

I'll be available for debriefing once the Wozniak brings us back to Earth.

SUBSPACE TRANSMISSION

HISTORY

Though the Corps of Engineers has a prestigious place in Starfleet at present, this was not always the case. In fact, the Corps had something of an inauspicious beginning as the construction crew assigned to build Earth's first starbase in the 2150s. The crew impressed the Admiralty with their ingenuity and efficiency when they completed and brought the base online days ahead of schedule. Their efforts were rewarded by keeping the crew together for future projects as the founding roster of the Starfleet Corps of Engineers.

Despite an increase in the 23rd Century of the SCE's mandate and numbers — with both civilian and Starfleet personnel — thanks to the expansion of the Federation and the growing number of starbases being built in Federation space, the SCE was often under-equipped. The scarcity of resources along a then-unexplored frontier meant the SCE lost out to the Fleet's exploration and defensive work. The engineers had to rely largely on their skills and talent for innovation to perform their tasks. Though the Corps was able to convince Starfleet Command that it required increased mobility and its own dedicated starships (rather than relying on transport via vessels assigned to other mission profiles), Fleet Operations felt the fleet was too overworked to give the SCE newer ships. Instead it restored previously decommissioned vessels for their use, primarily Daedalus-class starships, a class that was entirely retired in 2196 and individually difficult to restore thanks to damage that many of vessels suffered during the Earth-Romulan War.

As the Corps of Engineers' accomplishments gained further acclaim — the ten-month endeavor to tunnel out the asteroid Regula for use by Dr. Carol Marcus' Genesis terraforming project — Starfleet Command expanded the SCE's operational resources. Teams were assigned to oversee most major construction projects or to give permanent billets on vessels and outposts where their expertise could prove useful. The SCE also continued their mobile operations aboard dedicated vessels, using smaller vessels such as Oberth-class research vessels until the 24th Century, when Fleet Operations began assigning the Corps newer ships such as Saber-class cruisers.

THE CORPS OF ENGINEERS IN PLAY

The Starfleet Corps of Engineers can be a valuable source of stories for a **Star Trek Adventures** campaign, as the Corps' efforts and projects throughout Federation space are potential subjects of interest to a Player crew. Player Characters may be called upon to aid the Corps in a

project or provide assistance if an unpleasant fate befalls an engineering team. If the ship or starbase on which the Player Characters serve suffered severe damage in battle, or experienced a catastrophic and crippling systems failure, the SCE would be dispatched to give them aid.

A Player Character may consider service within the Corps of Engineers as a previous posting to where they serve during the campaign. This provides several potential story seeds. The character may have had to leave the SCE under unpleasant circumstances: perhaps a failed mission, or a traumatic event the effects of which they have yet to overcome; the past has now, in some way, come back to haunt them. Players can use the Corps as a springboard for ideas during *Step 6: Career Events*, of Lifepath character creation (**Star Trek Adventures** *core rulebook,* p. 118). At the other end of the spectrum, perhaps the character was a valuable asset and a fond member of their previous SCE team and wanted their present posting for a simple change of pace: a mission could be centered on a reunion with their old Corps colleagues. Such a reunion may be complete happenstance, but form an integral backdrop of the session's main plotline, or perhaps the team contacted their former member (or vice versa) to help them with a problem that separately can't be handled, but together…

A STARFLEET ENGINEERING CAMPAIGN

A campaign can be centered on a Starfleet Engineering team with minimal adjustment to the standard campaign roles as defined in the core rulebook's *Chapter 5: Reporting for Duty*.

A typical SCE team consists of a commanding officer (usually of commander rank), an executive officer (one rank below the commanding officer at best), and the rest of the team billets filled with any number of enlisted engineers or scientists serving subordinate roles. While most Corps personnel belong to the operations division, the Corps has command and science division personnel in its ranks, so Players may create characters of any of the three divisions provided they develop them with Discipline levels, Focuses, and Talents appropriate and valuable to a campaign with an engineering theme.

Mobile teams assigned to dedicated Starfleet Engineering starships are usually separate from the ship's crew. Some teams do hold crew positions in addition to their SCE duties: for example, the team's commanding officer could double up as the ship's executive officer or chief engineer, or their ship's second officer, or hold a crew position in line with their area of expertise. If the SCE team and their ship's crew are separate, the Players may create a mix of characters from either the ship's crew or the SCE team; center their group on either the crew or the team; or play one group as Main Characters and the other as Supporting Characters. The team can also be supplemented by security and medical personnel when needed, either assigned to the team by Starfleet Engineering or seconded from the ship's crew.

Ship-based SCE teams were only prevalent in the Original Series and *The Next Generation* are typically assigned to smaller ships no larger than Scale 4, usually vessels of either the *Daedalus* class (pre-2280s), *Oberth* class (2280s and later), or *Saber* class (2370s and later). Since the

Corps was typically assigned older and even previously decommissioned ships up until the 2280s, the Players' ship may have Traits such as Long-Serving to reflect the ship's age, and refits (depending on its age). You may also wish to deny the Players' vessel refits, forcing them to upgrade their starship through Character Development (*Star Trek Adventures* core rulebook, p. 138), or as the basis for a storyline to find particularly rare refit components.

Starbase-embedded engineering teams were prevalent in all eras of play and are structured much in the same way those for ship-based teams. The main difference is that SCE detachments on starbases were larger in number than ship-based teams, sometimes twenty or more, so the Gamemaster should generate a few NPCs to fill out the team's ranks in addition to the Player Characters.

OPERATIONS DIVISION
SECTION 31

"WE DEAL WITH THREATS TO THE FEDERATION THAT JEOPARDIZE ITS VERY SURVIVAL.
IF YOU KNEW HOW MANY LIVES WE'VE SAVED, I THINK YOU'D AGREE THAT THE ENDS DO JUSTIFY THE MEANS."

— LUTHER SLOAN

UNDER NO OFFICIAL LISTING

You need to know that by telling you this, I am putting you and your family in danger. But no one else will believe me, or they are part of it too, I can't be sure anymore. I don't know who I can trust, or if I can even trust anyone, but I can't do this alone. So, this is what I know, what few lies and half-truths I've been able to put together. I'm sorry to make you a part of this, because now there is no going back.

Outside any official listing and unnamed on any intelligence report, is one section of Starfleet Intelligence that few people know about. It operates under layers and layers of shadow, never showing its true hand and ruthlessly defending its secrets. That department is only known as "Section 31" and it is responsible for a host of black operations and off-book

missions that would make anyone who knew about them doubt everything the Federation claims to stand for. It takes its name from Article 14, Section 31 of the Federation Charter which allowed "extraordinary measures to be taken in times of extreme threat". But it is unclear if that section allowed the creation of the organization, or it just uses that as a justification for its actions.

It is all very well for Starfleet Intelligence to declare it is going to play by the rules and not do anything illegal or immoral in the pursuit of intelligence. But Section 31 believes that only its existence makes that possible. You think the Romulans or the Cardassians are going to play nicely just because the Federation has decided to hobble its operatives? No, they will see the Federation for what it is — weak. Those outside the espionage game can talk all they like about what is right, but there are forces out there that threaten the very existence of the Federation. They will use any means necessary to destroy everything it has built. And you need to be ready to fight fire with fire. That is Section 31, the monster in the shadows that keeps the Federation safe, the assassin with blood on their hands so the Federation stays clean.

That at least is what Section 31 operatives believe, and how correct they are depends very much on your point of view. Are these rogue agents who endanger the heart and soul of the Federation? Or are they its valiant protectors, ready to do what must to be done, even if it costs their own souls, to keep it safe? The Section 31 operative will tell you they have protected the very existence of the Federation on several occasions, but they will never tell you how because that information is classified. So, who can you believe? All that is clear is that they operate outside Federation law and are prepared to commit all and any despicable acts to fight an intelligence war that may be as threatening as their paranoid fantasies lead them to believe.

Morality and the truth become very, very muddy when it comes to Section 31. However far you are prepared to go, it may not be enough. Are the threats they see real, or are they the delusions of those who desperately want to justify their terrible actions? Every Section 31 agent has two nightmares. One is that they will not be willing to do whatever dreadful thing they need to do next. The other is that all the awful things they have done were not necessary at all.

And remember, we never had this conversation.

HISTORY AND ORGANIZATION

Everything connected to Section 31 is so cloaked in secrecy, that it is very hard to really know where the organization came from, how it organizes itself or who is involved. In fact, the surer a fact, the more likely it is the information is false. Section 31 works hard to spread disinformation about its operatives and operations, and makes it hard work to uncover these lies so they are all the more convincing. Section 31 agents have died just to maintain the lies about the organization.

The organization likes to hide in plain sight and have made sure that the term "Section 31" appears occasionally in official classified Starfleet operations. Such references are usually for minor secret projects, the sort of thing that is restricted information but not all that important. In this way, when someone suggests they have found a rogue organization called Section 31, the admiral they inform is already aware of a Section 31 whose operations are classified but not in question (such as a secret section of an archive). The admiral in question then considers the issue to be nothing more than the result of an overzealous and overexcited, but under-informed, officer and dismisses the problem. Unable to deny

the existence of this false "Section 31" and equally unable to reveal its existence as it is still classified, most admirals end up forced to neither confirm or deny the existence of a Section 31. They then appear to be working for Section 31, even though they still don't really know what it is, adding another layer to the conspiracy theory.

It is generally assumed that the roots of Section 31 go back to the time of transition when humans began to form and lead a new Federation. To many people, giving up their sovereignty to serve the benefit of several new and alien worlds was just too much. Many in the intelligence community found the transition even more difficult. Having made a career of paranoia and suspicion, few were ready to trust their new neighbors and allies who had recently been strangers. As noted before, many also felt the Federation party line of always taking the moral high ground to be not only naïve but potentially self-destructive.

The old guard of spies found there was no place for them in the new order. The world they operated in was being taken apart and all their secrets exposed. Some simply retired, but others could not walk away from what they saw as their duty. As agents found like minds, they began to work across the sections where they had found themselves. Ironically, this level of cross departmental cooperation, even among what were technically rogue agents, would never have been possible in the "good old days".

As time passed, and the Federation became more of what it aspired to be, the rogue agents and their inheritors found their operations harder and harder to maintain. As each of them were found out or overplayed their hand, the rest dug themselves even deeper into the Federation intelligence network. In time, they were so deeply entrenched they were almost impossible to find and even harder to remove.

There is very little formal organization to Section 31. On one hand, it appears to have a dedicated leadership ordering missions to construct their own new world order. At the same time, it appears its true agents are simply working on their own plots that simply advance a shared "Section 31" agenda. It is quite possible there is no one in charge of Section 31: after all, under the layers of secrecy it would be very easy to send false information to its operatives.

It's likely, therefore, that Section 31 operates a very flat hierarchy. There are no leaders or followers, only operatives. Operatives can vouch for others they know as they either recruited, or were recruited by, their fellows. This makes them the only people they can trust where Section 31 is concerned. No one in Section 31 truly knows how many operatives exist. Given the small size of each known group, operatives can communicate with each other and form plans together, being careful not to interfere with each other's designated jurisdiction. Operatives might be given control of an area but might just as easily be the operative for blackmail operations, the assassination operative, or simply run Romulan or Klingon operations. Each operative is usually given jurisdiction over an area they are especially skilled in (such as an expert in Romulan culture being given control of all operations involving Romulans). Once an area is assigned, the operative keeps it forever and it becomes their life's work.

Given how complicated Section 31 plans usually are, each operative gives his colleagues a wide birth. It would be very easy for plans to upset the carefully detailed work of another operative. It is also good for them to keep far from each other to ensure that if one of them fails the others are not likely to be caught as well. For this reason, operatives never meet (even through comms) in groups of more than four or five.

OPERATIONS

To maintain secrecy, Section 31 works almost exclusively through intermediaries. Anyone you meet who claims to be working for Section 31 is probably just another stooge. The real Section 31 agents keep their identities very secret, and often execute their useful underlings once they are finished with them.

Missions and operations for Section 31 are exceptionally varied, although that is just a polite way to say there is nothing they won't do if necessary. If charm works better than blackmail they'll try that first, but there are no lengths to which they will go to when pursuing an end. The end always justifies the means in Section 31. Always. Having said that, they prefer not to kill people or perform more brutal actions like blackmail, torture and kidnapping, but not because they have any moral qualms. Murder and sudden disappearances are messy and difficult to cover up: friends and relations look for people who disappear, blackmailed people might go to the authorities, etc. Section 31 likes to leave no trace, so the best policy is not to get their hands dirty. Still, if they can remove someone in such a way that no one will ever come looking and no one will find the body, they won't hesitate.

Section 31 operations are so subtle you might be forgiven for not even noticing they are happening. They don't usually perform midnight assaults on secret installations or build hidden battle cruiser fleets. Instead, Section 31 is about tipping the balance. They make one or two subtle changes to ensure that votes go their way or enemies lose their power. They might ensure the food at a reception contains something a delegate is a little allergic to, so they must retire and don't feel well enough to vote. Fomenting civil unrest on a faraway colony might force a government to commit its forces away from a facility Section 31 are targeting. A cartographical mistake on a new map makes sure certain territories are on a different side of a border, limiting the voting power of the local governor.

Apparently small changes, but with big consequences, are the preferred tactic. It is very difficult to even see the hand of Section 31 at work, and even when it has completed its mission, the purpose is often only clear much later. When observers backtrack through a chain of events, certain coincidences suddenly seem very fortuitous. But by then it is too late, and Section 31 has moved to another game.

Even when Section 31 uses other outside agents, it keeps its cards very close to its chest. This is mainly because the pawns they use could be squeamish about what might need to be done. Everything they ask their agents to do appears quite mundane and not especially immoral. They might ask someone to pick a child up from school and take the child home as normal, looking after them until they are collected. But, unknown to the agent, the place they take the child isn't the child's home and the sudden disappearance causes chaos. When the agent realizes what has happened, Section 31 then tells them they have another job. This time, if they refuse, they will be named to the authorities as a kidnapper…

Section 31 likes to offer its potential agents a choice. When someone comes to with an offer to help in return for a small favor, the agent can always walk away. If they do, there is no ill will. Section 31 may never bother them again. But… the favor is so easy, and the reward so desperately needed that most people agree to Section 31's suggestions. Unfortunately, once the choice is made, it is forever and there is no going back. Each mission carried out for Section 31 takes the agent deeper down the rabbit hole until they are steeped in guilt. And all because, at the first meeting, someone didn't say "No".

Every operation of Section 31 functions under layers of obfuscation. They never directly ask any co-opted agents to do whatever it is that needs doing. Instead, they give their chosen tools a job and leave them to get on with it, explaining nothing about why they need this service done. In many cases they might be banking on the agent to fail in the task. They may even have planned for the agent to balk at the last moment, screw up or even try to turn the tables. Even when this is known, it is hard to grasp what Section 31 are really hoping to achieve without more information. Until the big picture is understood, and why Section 31 need a person to work for them, there is little hope of figuring out their true motives and intentions. Section 31 likes to stay several steps ahead of all its agents, and it works hard to know everything about how a person will behave before putting anyone to work.

While this layer of shadow is a great defense, it can also be a weakness. Section 31 relies on remaining hidden, so exposure of its activities does great damage. It can only get away with doing despicable deeds because no one knows anything. Each time it is unveiled, the enormity of its actions is even harder to conceal. More to the point, Starfleet must root out Section 31 wherever it finds it, otherwise the existence of such a group will sully the Federation's reputation and damage its treaties and connections with other governments.

For all their secrecy, however, Section 31 must come out of hiding for one reason: recruitment. The Section only seeks out the best, and when a truly exceptional candidate appears only one of their own can truly make an assessment. Of course, an approach is never direct. Instead, Section 31 will recruit them at a distance for several operations to see if they have the skills and (more importantly) the right "immoral fiber" for the Section. Only when Section 31 is sure they want to make an offer do they meet a candidate directly and bring them inside.

THE TRUTH

The real story of Section 31 is a complete mystery. Only the Gamemaster can ever truly know what this secretive and exceptionally skillful group are really doing, or their true capabilities. Here we present a series of six different truths that might be the real story behind Section 31. The Gamemaster should choose one of the following options (or create their own truth) and keep it in mind as they use Section 31 in their campaign. While these will initially appear very similar to the Players, the one picked "truth" help the Gamemaster determine the scope and power of Section 31 and, more importantly, will determine who the Player Characters can turn to when they need to stand against it. Of course, there is nothing wrong with a Gamemaster changing their mind as the campaign progresses! After all, everything the Player Characters may have learned during the campaign may simply be disinformation, unless that is the purpose of any new information they learn...

A ROGUE AGENCY

This is the most common theory: that Section 31 is an illegal agency using Starfleet resources in secret to pursue an agenda that is against Starfleet and Federation policy. While it is deeply entrenched, Starfleet Intelligence actively seeks out its members and does its best to uncover their operations. It is slow going as even Starfleet Intelligence doesn't know who can be trusted. But if they find someone outside who has the right connections, such as the Player Characters, they might be able to take down the organization or infiltrate its heart.

A DENIABLE ASSET

While Starfleet Intelligence denounces the actions of Section 31, the organization is secretly a full part of Starfleet Intelligence. The higher levels of Starfleet Intelligence have not been eager to give up the darker aspects of espionage, so they created Section 31 to do the things they couldn't be seen to do. They can distance themselves from Section 31 if it is discovered. The hypocrisy of Starfleet runs deep here:

condemning Section 31 on one hand, and on the other secretly being the ones issuing the marching orders. However, the dream of the Federation is still important here: Starfleet Intelligence is prepared to sacrifice Section 31 to maintain its reputation and the faith of the various member worlds.

In this version the operations of Section 31 will also be less appalling. With orders coming from Starfleet Intelligence it may perform some dark deeds, but they will clearly be in the interests of the Federation and its citizens.

THE HEART OF THE FEDERATION

Section 31 is not only part of Starfleet Intelligence, it IS Starfleet Intelligence. It is actually the real inner circle running not only intelligence operations but the Federation itself. In this version the power of Section 31 is almost without limit, and the dream of the Federation is an outright lie. While it is careful to ensure that it maintains the reputation of the Federation, Section 31 has carte blanche to do whatever it pleases.

THERE IS NO SECTION 31

Section 31 doesn't exist. It is a convenient fantasy created by Starfleet Intelligence to distract moles and rogue agents. All its operations are designed to root out counter-espionage efforts and the darker deeds of other governments. Those it recruits are being identified as rogue agents, so they can be removed from Starfleet Intelligence. Most of the organization is illusion, with murders being only pieces of theatre and operations only rumor. If enemies are looking at Section 31 as the real player, they are not looking at what Starfleet Intelligence is really doing. Everything here is smoke and mirrors, and what is real becomes very difficult to determine.

THERE IS ONLY SLOAN

Section 31 has only one operative, a single rogue agent called Luther Sloan. He might have been recruited by a predecessor, who may have served a larger Section 31 in the past (or it may have always been just one person). Sloan is a very experienced agent and possibly the most brilliant and talented spy of his time. Alone, he has compiled a vast amount of intelligence and has a deep understanding of the right way to apply it. He has created the fiction of a whole department around him to make others think there is more to Section 31, and to stop people being able to predict his reach. If Sloan is taken down, then there is no Section 31.

AN OBSIDIAN ORDER OR TAL SHIAR PLOT

Finally, what if the masters of Section 31 are not part of the Federation? Perhaps the Cardassians or Romulans inserted their own agents into the nascent Federation and use Section 31 as their cat's-paw? Even worse, perhaps it is a joint *Tal Shiar* and Obsidian Order operation! In which case, who is really running it now and can they trust each other?

Perhaps this rogue agency has even gone rogue from its original masters. In which case, who does it serve now? The Federation? The Romulans? The Cardassians? Section

31 itself? Perhaps the Section is actually a front for a joint operation by all the Galaxy's intelligence services to ensure they control the destiny of the Alpha and Beta Quadrants rather than their respective governments? Maybe the Klingons are in charge, or even the Borg. This would be so out of character for either species… but maybe that's what they want you to think. Paranoid? Paranoid? Is anyone paranoid enough?

SECTION 31 IN PLAY

With all this intrigue and cloak and dagger shenanigans, Players will probably be wondering how they can join Section 31, but if they are asking are they fit to be Federation officers? True, Section 31 is privy to incredible secrets and believes it serves the Federation, and a life in Section 31 is full of espionage and adventure. For all its "cool factor" Section 31 is a canker in the Federation's rose: its moral corruption may initially appear to be expedient, but it is a morality flies in the face of everything the Federation represents. It is a danger to the Federation's reputation, because how can the Federation insist it practices what it preaches when it allows Section 31 to operate? Luckily for the Federation, Section 31 recognizes this, hence the policy

of extreme secrecy. The fact remains that what it is prepared to do, and what it does, are not fitting for anyone who wears a Starfleet uniform.

Section 31 are the voices in the shadows. Its agents might be direct enemies, with the Player Characters trying to uncover Section operatives to purge the Federation of their influence. Yet they also work well as a secret contact that only ever wants a favor in return for valuable information. Every interaction with Section 31 agents as allies should slice away another small part of a Player Character's morality once they know what they are dealing with. Everything Section 31 does is corrupt, but they are a tempting friend all the same. How long will it be before the Player Characters realize they are tied to something that stands against everything they vowed to protect and serve?

If a Player Character learns of Section 31's existence it is usually because the organization is thinking of recruiting them. Such situations are rare: while Starfleet only accepts the best and brightest, Section 31 only accepts the best of Starfleet. Beyond that, a recruit must be dedicated to the Federation, but also prepared to betray everything they believe in to maintain the security and safety of the Federation. It is a rare combination, so it is more likely that any potential "recruitment" is only being done so the Player

Character can be used as a stooge in one of Section 31's plans. After all, when it all goes wrong, a character claiming they were only doing what they told so that they could join an illegal organization will be a particularly weak excuse for a Starfleet officer to make. Always assuming they survive to go to trial…

If Player Characters do get involved with an actual Section 31 mission, they will be hard pressed to realize it. Only after careful consideration of the mission's ramifications will they see the hand of Section 31. Any missions will appear simple but often prove difficult in execution: often this is because Section 31 knows that events are likely to become complicated and purposely does not pass on this useful information. It prefers to leave agents in the dark, as understanding the big picture is what Section 31 does, not the agents. Everything is carefully calculated, and the Gamemaster should feel free to make events work out in Section 31's favor regardless of the mission's result or spend Threat to do so. Whatever the Player Characters do, Section 31 predicted their actions and those actions were the plan all along!

True recruitment is tailored to the recruit in question. There is no new background or skill set required. If Section 31 thinks they have a use for a person's skills and (more importantly) their attitude, it will test them and bring them in if everything checks out. Once in, an agent is there for life, and failure or retirement will see the character quietly disappear. If a Player Character wants to join Section 31, it is entirely up to the Gamemaster to decide if they meet the standards required. Joining Section 31 is not a character generation option but the result of a long campaign.

The best way is to decide that a Section 31 operative is observing the Player Character over a few missions to see if they are worth approaching. But both the Player and character will never know they are being observed or tested. Should they manage to join the Section, it must be understood that the Player Characters may have to be retired as an NPC as they go deeper into the shadows. They won't get to serve with the same crew, as anyone who knows the Player Character may see a change in their business and routine. They will usually be kept in Starfleet but reassigned to a new crew when required. Eventually they will simply work beyond any Starfleet cover and remain in the shadows.

Even with all their potential complexity, a Gamemaster may be tempted to run a campaign set within Section 31. Such campaigns will need to be especially involved: Section 31 works so secretly that its hand is never seen even after it has completed its objective. It also expects its operatives to be especially competent and able planners so the Gamemaster could leave the construction of missions to the Section 31 Player Characters. They should come up with a situation they wish to twist to their advantage, listing the various characters and locations involved in what they intend to do. The Gamemaster then only needs to make sure things get complicated, taking their mission design and twisting the truth of it to make their carefully constructed plan more difficult. If things get too complicated, the mission may change to being about how the Player Characters escape (and hide their involvement) rather than succeed. And remember: for Section 31, the only truly successful mission is one that no one ever, ever knows about.

TEMPORAL INVESTIGATIONS INTERVIEW

TRANSCRIPT 325467

"So, Lieutenant, let's try this again. Did the cup break?"

"What do you mean?"

"It's a simple enough question. You mention in your report that you broke a cup in your quarters but later found it unbroken. Is this correct?"

"I'm not sure."

"Well, be sure."

"I'm sorry, but we were under attack by three Cardassian battleships. I wasn't really worrying about the crockery in my quarters."

"Sit down lieutenant and answer the question."

"We are on the brink of war with the Cardassians after that encounter; don't you want to ask me something important?"

"This is probably the most vital fact in the whole affair. Are you aware we detected chroniton particles across your ship, including your quarters?"

"No, but I fail to see…"

"These particles are a sign of temporal disturbance, and we suspect a time agent may have been in play during the encounter. Only those caught in the temporal wake will be aware of any changes to the timeline, and, no matter how small, those changes allow us to piece together the movements and actions of that agent."

"But outright war was averted, so what is the problem?"

"The problem, lieutenant, is that we don't know if that agent saved us from a potential war, or was responsible for nearly causing one. And if we don't uncover their agenda there will be nothing to stop them trying again."

CHAPTER 03.00

OPERATIONS DIVISION CHARACTERS

2657890
49029472546891

03.10	SECURITY SCHOOL	036
03.20	ENGINEERING SCHOOL	044

OPERATIONS DIVISION CHARACTERS
SECURITY SCHOOL

"YOU'RE GOOD AT BUILDING THINGS, I'M GOOD AT BLOWING THEM UP."

— LIEUTENANT MALCOLM REED

PROTECTING THE FEDERATION

When exploration and scientific discovery brings beings of the Federation face to face with hostile forces — and diplomacy fails — it is officers of the security branch of Starfleet that are called upon to protect their shipmates, and the rest of the Federation, from violence and destruction.

While Starfleet's mandate is to seek out new life and new civilizations, it is modeled after a military organization and quickly reverts to its roots as a naval force to defend those that cannot defend themselves. Without this, often unpopular, truth the Federation would have fallen to its enemies generations ago. Despite its efforts to distance itself from the idea of being "military", Starfleet relies on those officers who specialize in protecting the security of the Federation to engage in both ship and ground based combat operations when needed.

Because of this, security officers are the most likely to maintain (and expect) a certain readiness to fight, to keep a cool head during emergencies, and to respect the chain of command.

When not engaged in combat operations the officers belonging to the security and tactical sections of operations are responsible for peace keeping, law enforcement and emergency response aboard Starfleet vessels and stations and on countless Federation worlds. Thankfully, crime within the Federation is infrequent, and most law enforcement efforts are focused on smuggling, piracy and organized crime from non-Federation groups operating within Federation space.

The most common duty aboard ship for these officers is at the tactical stations. All graduates of the security track are skilled in the use of phasers, torpedoes and tractor beams, along with deflector and defensive shielding systems. In addition, they are educated in the basic scientific principles

PERIODS OF CONFLICT

Below is a list of key (not all) conflicts from the 22nd–24th century involving United Earth or the Federation. This gives a good idea of periods of tension to use in a game of *Star Trek Adventures* focused on security storylines:

WAR	DATE	BELLIGERENTS	
Xindi Crisis	2153–2154	United Earth, Andorian Empire	Xindi
Earth-Romulan War	2156–2160	United Earth, Vulcan, Andorian Empire, Tellar Prime	Romulan Star Empire
Federation-Cardassian War	2347–2367	United Federation of Planets	Cardassian Union
Federation-Tzenkethi War	2360s	United Federation of Planets	Tzenkethi Coalition
Federation-Klingon War	2372-2373	United Federation of Planets, Bajoran Republic, Cardassian Union	Klingon Empire
Dominion War	2373-2375	United Federation of Planets, Klingon Empire, Romulan Star Empire, Bajoran Republic, Cardassian Liberation Front, Cardassian Union (2375)	Dominion, Cardassian Union (pre-2375), Breen Confederacy, Son'a

ENLISTED SECURITY TRAINING

Characters who attend the Starfleet Technical Services Academy can be created using the creation in play rules (*Star Trek Adventures core rulebook, p. 131*). However, if you wish to use Lifepath creation follow these instructions:

During *Step Four: Starfleet Academy*; a character may select the **Enlisted Service Track** instead of the traditional Starfleet Academy tracks.

- The character gains a single Value, which should reflect some aspect of the character's beliefs developed during that training.

- The character gains 3 points to increase Attributes, which may be split between two or three Attributes (increase three by +1 each, or one by +2 and a second by +1). The character may select these Attributes freely.

- Characters gain +1 Conn, +2 Security, +1 Engineering to their Disciplines

- Characters gain the Chain of Command Focus. Then they may select two additional Focuses.

- Characters gain a single Talent.

- Characters also gain the "Enlisted Crewman" Trait. Enlisted personnel use the enlisted ranks (*Star Trek Adventures core rulebook, p. 127*) instead of the commissioned officer ranks. Characters with the Untapped Potential Talent and the Enlisted Service Trait may not have a rank above petty officer (3rd class). Characters with the Veteran Talent and the Enlisted Service Trait must be either chief petty officer or chief warrant officer rank.

During the game, when a character with the Enlisted Service Trait would be eligible for a promotion, the Player and the Gamemaster may decide that the character has earned a commission. Instead of advancing to the next enlisted rank the character instead becomes an ensign and loses the Enlisted Crewman Trait.

---

that govern the use of these, including the design and construction of the various systems that keep them operational. This is not to say that security officers can perform complex maintenance or repairs; that is the task of the engineering department. Most security officers have a passing familiarity with how their systems work and what is required to keep them online.

STARFLEET SECURITY

Since the formation of Starfleet, when under the United Earth government, Starfleet Security has protected Starfleet vessels, facilities and human worlds. It handles major law enforcement, defense, security, and ground-based combat operations. It is headquartered at the Fleet Operations Center in San Francisco. While Starfleet Security officers are often under the immediate command of the senior and commanding officers of their assigned ships and bases, all officers also receive orders and operational directives from Starfleet Security.

While most officers and staff assigned to Starfleet Security are graduates of the Operations track Security course at the Academy, there are also medical and command staff assigned as Security support. Much like the other parts of Starfleet, such postings are often temporary and count as shore duty for fleet officers. Flag Officers are also assigned to Starfleet Security and, under most normal circumstances, serve in Security for several years. Starfleet Security is under the command of Fleet Operations, and Starfleet Command

appoints the Chief of Starfleet Security, the supervising officer in overall command. The Chief of Starfleet Security reports to both the head of Starfleet Operations and, during periods of heightened concern or conflict, directly to the President of the Federation.

LIFE ON THE FRONT LINE

Starfleet has been engaged in combat operations, at some level, nearly continuously for the last century, something that is not surprising given the variety of hostile governments and organizations scattered throughout the Alpha and Beta Quadrants. For most of these fights, the officers of Starfleet Security have been enough, and there has been no need to further expand into a standing military force. On rare occasions, however, a situation exceeds Starfleet Security's capabilities and resources, and additional support is needed.

Starfleet Security is the most likely branch to utilize enlisted service members within its operational areas. In fact, a significant portion of men and women within security are active or former enlisted. This becomes particularly true during periods of extended conflict with neighboring powers when a large force is needed to protect the Federation. These enlisted members of Starfleet do not receive the education of full officers. The typical enlisted crewman attends Starfleet Academy for their first year, where they study basic starship operations and tactical training, then transfers to the Technical Services Academy on Mars to finish their studies.

TACTICAL ROLES

When Starfleet deploys its officers and enlisted crewmen into conflict zones the standard practice is to organize them as five to ten-person teams called combat squads. Normally, each combat squad is led by a senior enlisted non-commissioned officer, or a junior officer. However, in the chaos of immediate battle, it is not uncommon for senior officers to be caught up in the fighting, and in such cases they assume command.

The practice of using combat squads is not unique to the Federation. Nearly all species follow a similar, if not identical, organizational structure. This is because the members of a combat squad provide expertise in a critical field or skill set that complements and enhances the effectiveness of their team mates, a concept known as "force multipliers." Unlike normal roles, these roles only function while the character is serving in a combat squad, and they do not prevent a character from also serving in one of the roles presented in the *Star Trek Adventures* core rulebook, or other *Star Trek Adventures* supplement.

A character may only benefit from a single role during any given scene. If a character is filling multiple roles the

Player must decide at the start of the scene which role their character is filling. Lastly, with the exception of the Squad Leader role, a combat squad may have any number of characters filling and benefiting from the following roles:

- **Squad Leader:** Each combat squad must have one leader. This character serves as the commanding officer for the team. *When using the* Direct *Task, the Squad Leader may assist using their Security Discipline, in place of Command. In addition, this Task is considered to have used the Command Discipline for all purposes.*

- **Explosive Ordnance Expert:** Due to the prevalence of explosives in major conflict zones, someone capable of using and deactivating these weapons is critical. *The character may reroll a d20 when attempting any Task involving a device or piece of equipment with either the Area Damage Effect or Grenade Quality.*

- **Combat Engineer:** From breaching security doors to erecting makeshift bunkers, combat engineers are responsible for dealing with all manner of fortifications (both enemy and friendly). They also make sure the squad's equipment is in good working order. *When the character succeeds at an Engineering Task during a combat encounter, they generate 1 bonus Momentum.*

- **Field Medic:** Every combatant's best friend is their medic. These characters are responsible of patching up their squad mates and keeping them alive in the heat of battle. *The character ignores any increase in Difficulty to the* First Aid *Task, related to the chaos or distractions of battle.*

- **Heavy Weapon Specialist:** Starfleet attempts to avoid lethal engagements but sometimes there simply isn't another way. In such situations, heavy weapon specialists ensure that their combat squad can match their opponent's firepower. *The character reduces the Escalation Cost of all weapons by 1, to a minimum of 1.*

- **Reconnaissance:** Throughout history, it is often the force with the most information that achieves its tactical objectives. Recon Characters are the eyes and ears of the team, venturing out ahead of the others to gather information. *Characters in the reconnaissance role generate 1 bonus Momentum that can only be spent to Obtain Information when they succeed at a Task using Insight or Security.*

PLAYING SECURITY CAMPAIGNS

Like all Disciplines, Security covers a broad range of training and abilities. First and foremost, it is the Discipline that covers nearly all forms of personal combat, including unarmed, melee and ranged attacks, and setting up or detecting ambushes and identifying adequate cover. Security also covers infiltration, stealth, bypassing and overriding lockouts, and all manner of other clandestine skills. In addition, this is the Discipline used for various law enforcement challenges such as tracking suspects, conducting forensic analysis, interrogation and so on.

Because of the variety of Tasks that Security can be used for, there are nearly an endless number of scenarios and campaigns that can be based around characters with high Security. The first and obvious choice is games that take place during periods of intense conflict. While the year 2371 could be thought of as a "calm before the storm", the build up to the Dominion War leaves many opportunities for characters to defend the Federation. Likewise, both the *Enterprise* and The Original Series eras are periods of heightened conflict. Engagements between Starfleet and other major powers, such as the Xindi or Klingon Empire, are frequent.

These are not the only opportunities for characters with high Security to take center stage. As discussed, Security covers all manner of law enforcement. Games centered around Security could be set during any era, with Players assuming the role of law enforcement officers, investigating crimes and tracking suspects across exotic worlds.

Even if a campaign is not centered around such activities, characters with a high Security Discipline often become crucial contributors during investigations. Their experience and training allows them to uncover clues and connect events, then form working theories that provide insights into situations that other characters may miss.

SECURITY IN PLAY

Each Discipline is an important part of a character's makeup but what it signifies for any given individual can vary. This section looks at what the Security Discipline may mean

MACO

Prior to the formation of the United Federation of Planets, Starfleet operated under the United Earth government. United Earth continued to maintain a standing military as Starfleet at the time was not intended to perform combat operations despite being armed. Of the various military branches, the Military Assault Command Operations (or MACO) was widely considered the best equipped and best trained force within Human space.

While they were separate organizations with dramatically different operational mandates, MACO and Starfleet grew to work closely together following the deployment of the Humanity's first warp 5 capable ship, the *U.S.S. Enterprise* NX-01. Almost immediately after setting out on its maiden voyage, the *U.S.S. Enterprise* came into conflict with several hostile cultures. This necessitated the coordination of United Earth's military resources, including Starfleet, and it became common for Starfleet vessels to host MACO detachments.

MACOs received the most advanced combat training and equipment available, and in the mid-22nd century they were at least a few years ahead of Starfleet. Training took place at numerous facilities within the Sol System, including Jupiter Station and Luna. Unlike Starfleet, which used traditional naval ranks, MACO used the ranks of the old United States Army. Following the founding of the Federation, MACO and United Earth's other military forces were disbanded; military officers were offered commissions within Starfleet on a case-by-case basis. MACO characters are therefore only available during the *Enterprise* era, and only to Human characters.

Character creation for a MACO character can follow the normal Lifepath creation system. At Step Four, instead of attending Starfleet Academy the character attends West Point or a similar military college/academy. From a rules standpoint simply select the security division within the operations track and apply the associated benefits.

CREATING SECURITY CHARACTERS

The following are suggestions for Players creating Security department characters, usually the chief of security or chief tactical officer:

LIFEPATH STEP ONE

Any species can serve in a security role, though different species may have different approaches to solving challenges. Species that offer increased Fitness or Control will be especially effective security or tactical officers.

LIFEPATH STEP TWO

At this stage, the *Homeworld* and *Frontier Colony* options might improve Control, Fitness and Security, though Security can be improved later if another choice is made.

LIFEPATH STEP THREE

In step three, the *Starfleet* and *Agriculture or Rural*, both provide useful increases to the key Attributes and Disciplines for a security officer.

LIFEPATH STEP FOUR

At the Academy, the *Operations Track* with the Security major is the natural choice for a security character, providing a significant increase to Security, as well as three Focuses and a single Talent. All can shape the character's abilities.

LIFEPATH STEP FIVE

At this step, any of the options are viable depending on the Player's concept for the character. Young Officer lends itself well to inexperienced (or "green") characters fresh out of the Academy and ready for action. Conversely the Veteran Officer is an excellent choice for a "grizzled combat veteran" concept.

LIFEPATH STEP SIX

Here, a number of Career Events can increase Security although this is more to add character flavor, perhaps showing the events that led to a current rank and position or their experience with combat operations. The *Ship Destroyed, Death of A Friend, Serious Injury, Conflict with A Hostile Culture, New Battle Strategy,* and *Special Commendation* are all appropriate and reflect a hazardous, action-packed career.

LIFEPATH STEP SEVEN

With finishing touches, the character's Attributes and Disciplines can be fine-tuned to fit a particular vision. Once complete, select a role. This is likely to be the chief of security, chief tactical officer, or any of the other roles discussed in *Life on the Front Line* (p.37).

to a character at especially high or low ratings. These are suggestions but they may help Players visualize a character and how Disciplines reflect their nature.

SECURITY SCORE OF 1

The character has only the most basic understanding of combat and tactics, and has difficulty identifying evidence or clues that could give answers to mysteries or crimes. They are likely uncomfortable with the notion of conflict and will likely give in to the flight side of a "fight or flight" moment. They will have difficulty surviving combat unscathed and are often more of a hindrance than help to their fellow officers when disruptor bolts fly. They may be uncoordinated, trip over ground clutter, be inaccurate with their phaser, or they may simply be cowardly and unable to withstand any intimidation or interrogation.

SECURITY SCORE OF 2 OR 3

The character is a capable fighter, able to defend themselves under most circumstances or operate the ships weapons systems with a fair degree of skill. They are able to avoid the notice of others when they want and, conversely, can track down individuals trying to avoid them.

SECURITY SCORE OF 4 OR 5

The character is an expert in ground and starship combat, able to defend themselves effectively. They can provide assistance and guidance to others, helping them survive the horrors of war. They are deadly warriors when they choose to be and have mastered multiple forms of combat engagements. They may be skilled tacticians, able to outwit their enemies and ensure minimal casualties. They may also be extremely effective investigators and be called upon to stop criminal activities, and be completely trusted to bring the guilty to justice.

OTHER DISCIPLINES

As a single Discipline can define a character's identity in a variety of interesting ways, combinations of Disciplines can also provide interesting context. The character's two highest Disciplines can be a definitive part of how they approach problems.

COMMAND

The character is a battlefield leader, a skilled tactician, an accomplished strategist, or a talented investigator. These characters lead away missions, fight battles, and deal with life-or-death situations. They tend to rise to prominence during times of strife and conflict, and are also likely to be physical, energetic individuals, accustomed to leading from the front.

Example: *Kira Nerys, a former Bajoran resistance fighter and Bajoran Militia major has command experience and is a capable soldier. Commander Riker earned numerous commendations during his meteoric rise for his instinctive*

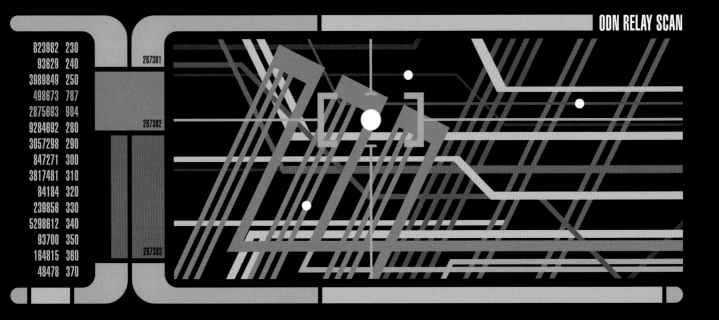

823982 230
93629 240
3989849 250
498673 787
2875693 984
9284692 280
3057298 290
847271 300
3817481 310
84184 320
239856 330
5298612 340
93700 350
164815 360
48478 370

287381

287382

287383

battle tactics while also proving himself to be a natural leader. Both are excellent examples of characters with high Command scores to complement their high Security Disciplines.

CONN

With knowledge of both starship operations, navigation, and ship weapons systems, the character can execute the most effective attack patterns and evasive maneuvers, and is also able to identify the critical systems to target on enemy vessels. High Conn also provides the character with an in-depth knowledge of Federation/Starfleet law and legal protocols, making them effective detectives.

Example: *Prior to his transfer to security, Worf served as a helmsman aboard the* U.S.S. Enterprise *NCC-1701-D. Several times he showed his skill as a capable pilot and warrior. Similarly, Ro Laren was a skilled pilot, but was also well known for her ability to conduct covert assignments.*

ENGINEERING

The character is an accomplished combat engineer, able to construct field fortifications and repair weapons and defensive systems, all while under enemy fire in the heat of battle. These individuals are equally comfortable in an engineering lab or when hunkered down next to rank-and-file soldiers. In addition, these characters are also experts in the design and development of improved starship weapon and shielding systems.

Example: *Chief Miles O'Brien was talented engineer, a decorated veteran of the Federation-Cardassian War, and was considered an expert in starship combat. Malcom Reed, the senior armory officer aboard NX-01 performed the duties of the ships tactical officer but also modified, improved and in some cases scratch-built weapon systems for the* U.S.S. Enterprise. *Both are characters who demonstrated high levels of Engineering and Security.*

SCIENCE

The character excels in situations where analyzing and applying scientific principles provides advantages in high stress conflicts. They can utilize environmental anomalies to their advantage, or discover a tactical advantage through hypothesis and theory testing. These characters often excel in forensic investigations and can derive information by examining evidence.

Example: *Sub-Commander T'Pol was instrumental in the success of the* U.S.S. Enterprise *NX-01 during its travels beyond United Earth space, applying her knowledge and expertise in various Sciences. However, she also served in the Vulcan Ministry of Security and undertook several successful missions for them.*

MEDICINE

Skilled combat medics (characters with high Security and Medicine) become every soldier's friend, and keep their crewmates alive. Such characters are even more important on the battlefield as they can contribute to the fighting and do not require escorts and protectors. When engaged in law enforcement, these individuals are often called on to serve as medical examiners and can gather crucial information by examining, for example, blood spatter and genetic samples or, in the most serious cases, examining the victim's corpse.

Example: *Dr. Julian Bashir served as the chief medical officer aboard Deep Space 9 but would eventually become involved with the secretive organization, Section 31, during the Dominion War. While he never became a full operative, his skills in covert operations were advanced enough to be offered a position within the group.*

SECURITY FOCUSES

This section provides a selection of Focuses that may be particularly useful or interesting for a security officer, and a brief discussion of what each Focus represents or how it could be used. Focuses are not necessary as a character can know about any of these areas of expertise without having an associated Focus. Having the Focus indicates an ability to gain 2 successes, when relevant, when rolling equal to or under the character's Security Discipline.

Deliberately, and as in real life, there is overlap between Focuses. Different fields of study and expertise inform one another, and individuals may develop similar skills from many starting points.

- **Criminal Organizations:** Despite the Federation's largely utopian society, organized criminal enterprises are a common feature in known space. Characters with this Focus are familiar with them. This Focus provides the character with detailed intelligence of organizations' inner workings, members, and common elements to criminal enterprises.

- **Fleet Formations:** Characters with this Focus are experts in starship fleet formations, including coordinated maneuvers, joint attacks, organized defensive patterns and so on. This Focus is common among flag officers and fleet liaison officers.

- **Forensics:** Characters with this Focus are highly skilled in analyzing crime scene evidence and deriving information from it. While most individuals can gather some information from a location, the same evidence speaks as clearly a subspace communique to characters with this Focus.

- **Hazardous Environments:** All Starfleet officers receive minimum training in hazardous environment survival. Characters with this Focus have the skills to survive and live as if they were on their homeworld rather than in a hazardous place. Combat veterans and survival experts are equally likely to have this Focus.

- **Martial Arts:** In an age where energy weapons are standard issue equipment the dedicated study of hand-to-hand combat has fallen out of favor. Characters with this Focus, however, have dedicated themselves to the mastery of one or more styles of martial arts, making them particularly dangerous opponents. The styles include aikido, karate, krav maga and *mok'bara*.

- **Small Unit Tactics:** A small force that is disciplined and well-organized can win in battle even when heavily outnumbered. Characters with this Focus are experts at forming and implementing offensive and defensive tactical plans for a small team.

- **Ship Engagement Tactics:** Tactical officers must be constantly vigilant and ready to advise their captains on the best way to engage an enemy if a situation turns hostile. This Focus provides the character with a vast knowledge of starship tactical maneuvers and the best counters for them.

- **Ship Lockdown Procedures:** In the event that an enemy manages to board a Starfleet vessel or there is a breach of internal security, the ship's security officers must contain the foe and prevent damage to vital internal systems. Characters with this Focus have extensive training locking down locations, trapping targets, or stopping movement throughout a ship, and know how to bypass such tactics.

- **Security Systems:** Often information or precious items require protection, and that is ensured through various security systems designed to prevent unauthorized access. These may take the form of particular devices or computer programs, and characters with this Focus are experts in all of them.

- **Targeting Systems:** Starship weapons are powerful and capable of devastating enemy vessels or planetary fortifications. Without effective targeting these systems are useless, and this Focus covers the sensors used to aim these weapons. The character understands their operation, maintenance and repair as well as the specially designed sensors used to acquire targets.

SECURITY TALENTS

This section provides additional Talents suited to security officers and characters with a high Security Discipline score. Each Talent may only be selected once unless otherwise noted. Players are free to rename the Talents they select to suit their own tastes and the backgrounds of their characters. This does not affect the rules for a Talent.

COMBAT MEDIC

REQUIREMENTS: Security 2+ and Medicine 2+
The character's abilities in field medicine and battle triage are exceptional and their presence inspires allies to continue any fight. Whenever the character attempts the *First Aid* Task (*Star Trek Adventures core ruebook* p. 174), they may spend one Momentum to cause the recipient to regain points of Stress equal to the numaber of the character's Medicine Discipline. A character may only regain Stress in this way once per scene.

CRIMINAL MINDS

REQUIREMENT: Security 3+
By imagining they are a suspect, and thinking in the same way, the character gains insight into a criminal's thought

processes or actions. Whenever a character succeeds at a Task to interpret information about a suspect using Reason, a character generates 1 bonus Momentum which may only be used for the *Obtain Information* Momentum Spend.

CRISIS MANAGEMENT

REQUIREMENTS: Security 3+ or Command 3+
Small squad tactics can mean the difference between life and death in a dangerous, hostile situation, and the character excels at coordinating action in battle. The character may make use of the *Direct* Task (***Star Trek Adventures*** *core rulebook* p. 173). If they already have access to the Direct Task, they may do so twice per scene instead of once.

DEADEYE MARKSMAN

REQUIREMENTS: Security 3+ and Control 10+
The character has spent time at the target range every day, working on their aim. When the character takes the *Aim* Minor Action (***Star Trek Adventures*** *core rulebook* p. 172), they reduce the Difficulty of their next Attack by 1, in addition to the normal effects of the *Aim* Minor Action.

FIRE AT WILL

REQUIREMENTS: Security 2+ and Daring 9+
The character is capable of tracking multiple targets and making attacks against them with great effect. Whenever the character makes a ranged weapon attack, and then uses the *Swift Task* Momentum spend to make a second ranged attack, they ignore the normal Difficulty increase from *Swift Task*.

FULL SPREAD — MAXIMUM YIELD!

REQUIREMENT: Security 3+
The character is skilled in setting up torpedo attacks. In addition to the normal benefits of a Salvo, the attack also gains the benefit of the *Devastating Attack* Momentum Spend as though 2 Momentum had been spent. The *Devastating Attack* Momentum Spend may not be selected again for this attack.

HUNKER DOWN

REQUIREMENT: Security 2+
Making good use of the surroundings for protection is one of the hallmarks of a skilled soldier. Whenever the character rolls Cover Dice (***Star Trek Adventures*** *core rulebook* p. 171), they may add +1 Resistance to the total for each Effect rolled.

LEAD INVESTIGATOR

REQUIREMENTS: Security 3+ and Conn 2+
The character has a mind intrigued by mystery and investigation, and is often called upon to review and coordinate response to lawbreaking. The character generates two bonus Momentum after a successful Task to investigate a crime.

MARTIAL ARTIST

REQUIREMENT: Security 4+
There are countless forms and styles of hand-to-hand combat, and the character has mastered several of them. The character's Unarmed Strike attacks gain the Intense Damage Effect. If the character also has the Mean Right Hook Talent, then both Damage Effect apply when Effects are rolled.

PRECISION TARGETING

REQUIREMENTS: Security 4+ and Conn 3+
Having extensive knowledge of ship systems and operations, the character can easily target specific systems when attacking an enemy vessel. When the character makes an attack that targets a specific System they may reroll 1d20 in their dice pool, and the attack gains the Piercing 1 damage effect.

OPERATIONS DIVISION CHARACTERS
ENGINEERING SCHOOL

"YOU WHAT?!?! — BUT THAT'S A COMPLETELY IMPROPER PROCEDURE! YOU CAN'T JUST DUMP THAT MUCH RAW ENERGY INTO A BRIDGE TERMINAL..."

— CHIEF MILES O'BRIEN

MAINTAINING THE FLEET

As one of the largest subgroups of operations, engineers shoulder the burden of keeping the ships, bases, and facilities of Starfleet in peak operating condition. Without these talented individuals, the awe-inspiring technological wonders that make life in the 24th Century possible would cease to function.

Starfleet engineers are renowned throughout known space as being the finest of any major power in the Alpha or Beta Quadrants. It is often these miracle workers that make the difference between success or failure in deep space. Starfleet Academy provides young cadets with the finest education in advanced technological studies, and even the newest officers from these programs are far better equipped to maintain the sophisticated system aboard a vessel than their Romulan, Klingon or Cardassian counterparts.

While most possess a specialization in one or two technological areas, all Starfleet engineers understand, and are capable of maintaining, repairing, designing and constructing any number of devices. These range from the simplest convenience and comfort items to massive power generation plants and the other critical ships systems that make the exploration of space possible.

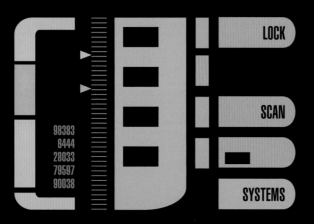

THE STARFLEET CORPS OF ENGINEERS

As one of the largest and oldest organizations of its kind, the Starfleet Corps of Engineers (SCE) consists of tens of thousands of Starfleet officers plus civilian scientists and engineers. It is tasked with overseeing fleet maintenance, new ship construction, decommissioning (or mothballing as it's sometimes called) outdated vessels and, most importantly, developing solutions to large scale engineering problems.

The Corps is to Starfleet engineers what the Federation Science Council is to Starfleet science officers, or the Admiralty is to those in the command department. Obtaining a duty assignment within the SCE can be very challenging for junior operations and engineering officers; the Corps tends to be very selective in the posting and filling of duty assignments (billets) within their ranks. A potential Corps engineer must have at least one published paper on a topic relating to the engineering sciences as their first qualification.

Acceptance by the SCE is often the only way for a Starfleet engineer to be promoted above lieutenant commander rank without transferring to the command branch. Captains within the SCE command SCE vessels, serve as supervising project directors, or run a sizable research and development team. The SCE is also authorized to promote technical staff to a flag rank. without the consent or approval of the Admiralty. SCE officers may only rise as far as rear admiral (upper half), and are not authorized to preside over active Starfleet vessels without a special dispensation from Starfleet Command.

The Corps also has billets for other Starfleet specialties as well, especially from the science division, though these tend to be restricted to those officers with backgrounds in engineering sciences such as structural metallurgy, theoretical physics and so on. There are postings for command officers within the SCE but these are almost always short-term postings, and commonly used as shore duty for fleet officers.

By the 24th century, operations has taken over from the science department in most day-to-day shipboard functions, freeing scientific group members to focus on their areas of study. In *The Next Generation* era it is rare to see a science officer assigned as a department head or among the senior staff. This is the case in both *The Next Generation* and *Voyager,* where the chief of operations acted as the senior science officer. *Deep Space Nine* was an exception: Jadzia Dax was a crucial member of Captain Sisko's team. However, when looking at the similarities between the series, Chief O'Brien, although

chief of operations served primarily as chief engineer, and Jadzia Dax had a role similar to that of Commander Data and Ensign Kim.

In earlier periods it was much more common to see a science officer serving as a senior staff member. This is probably due to the evolution of scientific study and understanding during the time between the different eras. During the 22nd and 23rd centuries, space was still largely unexplored and full of new, and often terrifying, anomalies. By the 24th century, many of these had been cataloged and studied, and Starfleet officers had some passing familiarity with their various natures. Because of this growth of understanding, a specialist science officer is often not necessary on the Bridge, and the position can be filled by an officer with a broader knowledge base.

OPERATIONS DEPARTMENT ABOARD A STARSHIP

Not every graduate from the Academy with an engineering background serves in the engine room. A significant number take postings in operations. These individuals become responsible for the day-to-day running of the internal systems and equipment aboard Starfleet vessels. They form the core of a starships crew and can be found working on every deck in nearly every compartment. It is their expertise in numerous systems that allows a ship to function.

Filling every role, from yeoman to deflector control operations department, members are responsible for large portion of the work done during a ship's mission. While not always glamorous or exciting, their efforts are no less critical to the overall success of each and every mission undertaken by the ship and its crew. In most circumstances, the members of operations department monitor and regulate ships internal systems and perform routine maintenance and repair. If a situation is beyond their capabilities or expertise engineering officers and crewmen are called for assistance.

The most visible member of the team is its department head: the chief of operations. Equal parts of scientist, engineer and operator, the chief of operations coordinates the activities of the officers and crewmen assigned to operations, and works with the chief engineer and the various groups within the science department.

On some Starfleet vessels, science officers may report up through the operations department to the chief of operations, instead of being set apart in their own department. This often occurs on smaller starships (Scale 3 or 4), where the small crew complement requires officers

UNIFORMS IN THE CORPS OF ENGINEERS

As the SCE is an affiliate group of Starfleet, officers within the Corps continue to wear standard Starfleet uniforms. Senior officers with the rank of commander or above are authorized to wear operations gold in place of command red. This is true even of the handful of flag officers within the SCE.

Civilians serving within the SCE wear either the standard grey jumpsuit common to members of the Federation Science Council or appropriate civilian business dress. Under most circumstances, the SCE director in charge of a civilian group has final say on what an acceptable dress code is for non-Starfleet personnel.

who can perform a variety of duty assignments. Operations keeps ships running. This is not to say that they are incapable scientists or engineers: far from it. Operations officers are often responsible for significant developments in the scientific fields, and the applied principles, that lead to technological innovation. Their career paths, however, often prevent them from delving deeply into any particular area of expertise. They can never hope to match the knowledge and experience of officers who have dedicated their careers to a single area of study.

Recognizing the value this brings to smaller Federation ships, Starfleet Academy provides an entire major within the operations track to prepare officers for this type of duty. Cadets within the ship operations track study a broad variety of topics, ranging from applied quantum mechanics to stellar navigation. Graduates from this major are expected to be

A character may instead choose to pursue a career within the **Ship Operations major**. This provides an additional selection within the *Operations Track*, with the following benefits:

- **VALUE:** The character gains a single Value as normal, which should reflect some aspect of the character's beliefs that developed during their time at the Academy.

- **ATTRIBUTES:** The character gains three points, which may be split between two or three Attributes (increase three Attributes by +1 each, or increase one by +2 and another by +1). The character may pick these Attributes freely, as normal.

- **DISCIPLINES:** The Player who selects the Ship Operations major gains +2 Conn, +1 Engineering, +1 Science.

- **FOCUSES:** The character selects three Focuses, at least one of which should relate to the character's chosen Track. Examples for ship operations track Focuses include: Computers, Electro-Plasma Power Systems, Flight Control Systems, Interrogation, Interstellar Navigation, Sensor Imaging, Transporters & Replicators.

- The character also gains a single Talent, which may be chosen freely.

The following are suggestions for Players creating engineering characters, usually the chief engineer or chief of operations:

LIFEPATH STEP ONE

Any species can serve in an engineering role, though different species may have different approaches to solving these challenges. Species that offer increased Reason or Control may be especially effective engineers.

LIFEPATH STEP TWO

At this stage, the *Isolated Colony* and *Starship or Starbase* options might improve Engineering, though Engineering can be improved later if another choice is made.

LIFEPATH STEP THREE

In step three, the *Starfleet*, *Business or Trade*, *Science and Technology,* and *Artistic and Creative* options can all increase Engineering, providing a Focus to help develop and specialize the character.

LIFEPATH STEP FOUR

The *Operations Track* with the Engineering major is the natural choice at the Academy for an engineering character. It provides a significant increase to Engineering, as well as three Focuses and a single Talent. All can shape the character's abilities.

LIFEPATH STEP FIVE

At this step, both the Experienced and Veteran Officer options are perfectly acceptable for a chief engineer, depending on the concept the Player has in mind for the character. It is possible for a Young Officer to serve in such a post, but this is very unlikely given the level of responsibility and expectation of the senior engineer aboard a Starfleet vessel except a small one.

LIFEPATH STEP SIX

Here, a number of Career Events can increase Engineering, although this is more to add character flavor, perhaps showing the events that led to a current rank and position. The *Special Commendation, Solved an Engineering Crisis*, and *Breakthrough or Invention* are all particularly applicable to engineering characters.

LIFEPATH STEP SEVEN

With finishing touches, the character's Attributes and Disciplines can be fine-tuned to fit a particular vision. Once complete, select a role: this is likely to be the chief engineer or chief of operations.

able to understand scientific theories and principles at work, apply them in practical applications through engineering, and then confidently and effectively operate the engineered systems in real time.

ENGINEERING IN PLAY

Each Discipline is an important part of a character's makeup, but what it signifies for any given character can vary. This section looks at what the Engineering Discipline may mean for a particular character. These are suggestions, but may help a Player visualize how Disciplines reflect their character's nature.

ENGINEERING SCORE OF 1
The character has basic training in electrical and mechanical systems, including a basic grasp of the differences between electrical, pneumatic, hydraulic and mechanical devices and some familiarity with their use. They know enough to perform basic operations and follow basic instructions, but are not likely to understand the theory behind these systems or why their work.

The character is unlikely to make more than basic repairs and is probably nervous in engineering spaces, and will be startled or confounded by the alarms and notifications of normal operations. Despite best intentions, the character is a hindrance rather than a help when assisting in operating or repairing complex systems. And worse, the character may believe they know more than they actually do, confusing or misusing basic operating principles from one system on another. In such cases, these characters may be more dangerous and distracting than other, more reserved, colleagues. A little knowledge is a dangerous thing...

ENGINEERING SCORE OF 2 OR 3
The character has a working knowledge of engineering and operational concepts, covering how various devices work, the scientific theory behind them, their practical applications, and repair. The character can competently disassemble, examine, fix, modify, and reassemble most devices and systems aboard a starship, though it may take an excessive amount of time. However, troubleshooting malfunctions across interlinked systems and developing a response is beyond their capability.

ENGINEERING SCORE OF 4 OR 5
At this level, the character is a skilled engineer, capable of quickly troubleshooting and repairing malfunctioning equipment, as well as designing and developing new technologies and enhancing existing systems beyond their original design specifications. The character is probably an

TALK LIKE A TECHNICIAN: THE USE OF TECHNOBABBLE

Technology in *Star Trek* is complex and works on scientific concepts and principles that are far beyond what the majority of Players and Gamemasters are knowledgeable in. Throughout the collected media, Starfleet officers discuss technology using terms that most Players are not going to know. Instead of expecting Players to study and memorize technical manuals and reference books that have been published over the years we've provided an easy way to talk like a Starfleet engineer. Anyone can do "technobabble"!

To use the Chart below simply gather and roll d20s and consult the chart below for technical new terms and concepts. Occasionally portions of the chart may not be applicable to the scene or circumstance. In that case simply omit that portion of technobabble!

ROLL	ACTION	DESCRIPTOR	SOURCE	EFFECT	DEVICE
1	refocus	microscopic	Quantum	flux	inhibitor
2	amplify	macroscopic	Positronic	reaction	equalizer
3	synchronize	linear	thermionic	field	damper
4	redirect	non-linear	Osmotic	particle	chamber
5	recalibrate	isometric	Neutrino	gradient	catalyst
6	modulate	multivariant	spatial	induction	coil
7	oscillate	nano	resonating	conversion	unit
8	intensify	phased	thermal	polarizing	grid
9	nullify	master	photon	displacement	regulator
10	boost	auxiliary	ionic	feed	sustainer
11	reverse	primary	plasma	imagining	relay
12	reconfigure	secondary	nucleonic	reciprocating	discriminator
13	actuate	tertiary	verteron	frequency	array
14	focus	back-up	gravimetric	pulse	coupling
15	invert	polynodal	nadion	phased	controller
16	reroute	multiphasic	subspace	harmonic	actuator
17	modify	emergency	baryon	interference	harmonic
18	restrict	tri-fold	tetryon	distortion	generator
19	reset	balanced	polaron	dampening	manifold
20	extend	oscillating	tachyon	invariance	stabilizer

acknowledged expert in several engineering specializations and may even be considered a leading light in their particular field.

It is characters of this level that have given birth to the reputation of Starfleet engineers being able to do nearly anything technologically conceivable. Starfleet engineers of this caliber think beyond standard maintenance and technical manuals, and develop new and creative uses for existing devices or combine commonly available equipment into new and interesting contraptions that often demonstrate impressive characteristics that their source materials didn't display.

OTHER DISCIPLINES

While a single Discipline define a character's identity in interesting ways, combinations of Disciplines can provide a deeper context. The character's two highest Disciplines can be a definitive part of how they approach problems.

COMMAND

The character is an accomplished team leader and, organizes and inspires their fellow technicians to perform complex tasks and extensive repairs effectively and efficiently. Modern starships have engineering departments with dozens (if not more) of technical experts in many fields. It is the team, section or department leaders that ensure expertise is properly assigned.

Example: *Benjamin Sisko spent several years leading starship development teams at the Utopia Planitia Fleet Yards. He is an example of a character with high Command and high Engineering, during at least part of his career. Similarly, Montgomery Scott and Charles 'Trip' Tucker III are engineers and capable leaders, and both took command of their respective ships when required.*

CONN

The character is not only an expert in building and maintaining the technological marvels aboard starships, but is equally at home operating them. This understanding of the use of ship's systems as well as how they are built is especially effective for starship engineers. These characters can often identify flaws and inefficiencies in systems they maintain by the "feel" of the ship and how it performs, rather than by relying on a technical readout or display.

Example: *Lieutenant Commander Geordi LaForge was one of the Enterprise-D's helmsmen prior to transferring to engineering and assuming the duties of the chief engineer. Lieutenant Nyota Uhura was a highly respected communications officer aboard the U.S.S. Enterprise during its historic five-year mission. During this time, she became an expert in the operation of the ship's communication systems but also was extremely familiar with protocols, languages and cultures throughout known space. Both characters showed a high degree of Conn as well as Engineering.*

SECURITY

The character is an accomplished combat engineer, able to construct field fortifications, as well as repair weapons and defensive systems, and do all that in the heat of battle. These individuals are comfortable in an engineering lab and "in the mud and trenches" holding a position with ordinary soldiers. In addition, these characters are also experts in the design and development of improved starship weapons and shielding systems.

Example: *Montgomery Scott was never an officer to back down from a fight, and often demonstrated a flair for getting malfunctioning ship's phasers to work in moments of crisis in numerous dangerous encounters for the U.S.S. Enterprise.*

SCIENCE

The character has a need to implement some practical aspect of a scientific discovery, but also wants to explore the theoretical aspects as well. It is these individuals that push the boundaries of what technology can achieve, always experimenting and tinkering to uncover some new phenomenon and deliver it to their fellows. Advancements in sensors, propulsion systems and nearly everything else would not be possible without these curiosity-driven people.

Example: *Lieutenant Commander Data and Ensign Harry Kim served as the operations manager on their respective ships. This duty required them to be accomplished engineers*

but also to be experts in various sciences, as neither ship had dedicated science officers amongst the senior staff. To perform these duties successfully, each possessed high Engineering and Science Disciplines.

MEDICINE

The character has in-depth knowledge of, and training in, bioengineering. These characters often work on the development of cybernetic limbs, sensory organ replacement, or artificial internal organs such as hearts, livers and kidneys. While they may or may not be present during surgery, they are frequently involved after an operation for calibration and adjustments. Engineers with a background in Medicine may also be crucial innovators in the field of medical technology.

Example: *Following the modification of his EMH programming, the Doctor aboard the starship Voyager incorporated an extensive database of technical and engineering principles allowing him to expertly modify his own program but also to respond to biological and technical emergencies.*

ENGINEERING FOCUSES

This section provides a selection of Focuses that may be particularly useful or interesting for an engineering officer, and a brief notes on each. Focuses are not necessary, as a character can know about any of these areas of expertise without having the associated Focus. Having the Focus indicates an ability to gain 2 successes when rolling equal to or under Engineering Discipline when the area of expertise is relevant.

There are overlaps between different Focuses. Fields of study often inform one another, and individuals may develop similar skills from different starting points.

- **Advanced Holograms:** The character is skilled in the design and programming of high-end functioning holograms and artificial intelligence. Once restricted to the realm of entertainment, hologram application has advanced considerably. The most notable example is the development of the Emergency Medical Hologram, and characters with this Focus are at the forefront of this work.

- **Cybernetics:** The character is knowledgeable of the ways that machines and technology can be directly connected to living beings. This includes not only artificial organs, which are common place by 23rd and 24th centuries, but also limb and sensory organ replacements. This Focus covers the medical procedures, various designs and replacement functionalities, as well as the construction, maintenance and repair of human-machine interfaces.

Diagnostics: Engineers constantly monitor systems to ensure they are operating at peak efficiency. Much like a medical doctor analyzing a patient's symptoms, the character is skilled at reviewing technical data and identifying areas of improvement or problems.

Electro-Plasma Systems (EPS): Nearly all known modern starship designs make use of a highly efficient power transfer medium known as Electro-Plasma. Characters with this Focus are experts in these systems and can ensure that critical systems remain online during normal and emergency operations. This technology has become so central to modern ship design that most vessels lack any other form of power transfer equipment.

Emergency Repairs: The character is skilled in damage control, the ancient (wet) navy term still used for making emergency repairs during battle or other dangerous situations. In the harsh environment of space, damaged or destroyed systems can become more dangerous than any enemy, and a character with this Focus is practically a wizard in this area.

Energy Weapons: While most engineers are more at home with propulsion systems, characters with this Focus have a deep expertise in high-energy weapon systems aboard ships and used by individuals. This includes the emission systems as well as target sensors, power feeds, energy vents and any other ancillary support equipment. This Focus would also include tractor beams, drilling, excavation, and various other energy-based construction equipment.

Flight Control Systems: Federation starships have very sophisticated navigation and conn systems, giving the ships highly effective and precise maneuverability. Engineers with this Focus are experts in maneuvering thrusters, reaction control systems, and the impulse maneuvering assemblies that provide vectored thrust from the impulse engines.

Imaging Equipment: Starfleet makes use of numerous kinds of imaging and display equipment. This Focus applies to the inner workings of viewscreens and work stations, but also applies to a host of medical equipment used to diagnose patients through internal images.

Impulse Fundamentals: While warp travel tends to receive a large amount of attention, it is impulse that moves the Federation at a local level. Almost every vessel utilizes some form of impulse engine for sub-light movement. This Focus covers the theory behind impulse engines, as well as the mechanical systems that make them work.

Jury-Rigging: Sometimes, the standard way of getting things done isn't enough. Characters with this Focus have a talent for finding creative ways to use technology to overcome problems. This Focus can be used anytime the character is attempting to make a device do something it wasn't designed to accomplish.

Modeling and Design: Before a piece of equipment, system or starship can be built it must be designed. This Focus applies to all manner of design and development processes. It can also come into play whenever the character is attempting to make experimental modifications to existing systems.

Reverse Engineering: Starfleet engineers are famous for their ability to adapt new technologies or integrate them into existing systems. Characters with this Focus display an intuitive understanding of any device they encounter, and have a near compulsion to integrate it into normal operations.

Sensor Calibration: When encountering new spatial anomalies, ships sensors are usually not set correctly to perform extensive and efficient analyses of the discovery. Characters with this Focus have extensive experience with modifying and calibrating sensors of all kinds to obtain the best quality of data possible.

Structural Engineering: Without strong foundations and well-designed frames, buildings and ships are fragile and ill-suited for the rigors of extended use. This Focus applies to all work done to develop and maintain structural integrity in all constructed objects from small habitats to orbital space docks.

System Maintenance: Characters with this Focus have extensive training and knowledge of the standard maintenance practices of Starfleet. They are comfortable working on everything from waste processing systems to phaser arrays. This Focus specifically covers standard maintenance and does not apply to modifications or repairs to systems.

Transporters/Replicators: Considered by many to be the greatest scientific development since warp drive, replicators allow the creation of nearly any conceivable object. Transporters provide reliable movement across planetary distances in moments. Characters with this Focus are recognized as experts in the field of matter-energy transmutation.

Troubleshooting: Often, engineering problems and system faults are not easily identifiable, or a there is a rare type of malfunction in a system. Characters with this Focus are naturals at tracking down system issues through trial and error. While such abilities are best applied to technical problems, characters with this Focus can often provide insights when assisting others.

- **Warp Core Mechanics:** Traveling at faster-than-light speeds requires more than simply plotting a course and turning on the engines. Characters with this Focus are recognized as experts in the field of warp core design, construction and use.

ENGINEERING TALENTS

This section provides additional Talents suited to engineers and characters with a high Engineering Discipline score. Each Talent may only be selected once unless otherwise noted. Players are free to rename any Talents they select to suit their own tastes and the backgrounds of their characters. As always, renaming does not change the rules for a Talent.

EXPERIMENTAL DEVICE

REQUIREMENTS: Main Character and Engineering 4+
You have designed and constructed a new piece of equipment that is either a brand new invention or is heavily modified from its original to the point of being barely recognizable. In either case, the device performs a function that you determine when you select this Talent. When used appropriately, it automatically provides you an Advantage. However, its experimental nature means there are lingering design bugs that sometimes plagues its function. Increase the Complication Range of any Task by 2 when using this device. This Talent may be selected multiple times with a different device for each selection.

EXPLOIT ENGINEERING FLAW

REQUIREMENTS: Engineering 3+ and Conn 3+
Following an ally's successful *Scan for Weakness* Task (***Star Trek Adventures*** *core rulebook,* p. 223), you may highlight an identified engineering flaw in the opponent's ship. In addition to the bonus granted by the *Scan for Weakness* Task, you may assist anyone making an Attack against the target ship, which does not count against the normal limit for providing assistance. If the Attack is successful, it generates 1 bonus Momentum. You must be able to communicate with the ally making the Attack to offer this assistance.

MAINTENANCE SPECIALIST

REQUIREMENTS: Engineering 3+
You are an expert in conducting and directing normal, day-to-day, maintenance and repairs on Starfleet equipment. Whenever they are required to perform maintenance, reduce the Difficulty by 1, to a minimum of 1, and halve the time required to complete the Task.

METICULOUS

REQUIREMENTS: Engineering 3+ and Control of 10+
You are patient, methodical, and check for errors before considering Tasks complete. Whenever they use Engineering to complete a Task, you may negate one Complication generated from the roll. However, during timed Tasks or Challenges, you take 1 more interval to complete the Task.

USS BENEVOLENT

CAPTAIN'S LOG, STARDATE 48512.3

We arrived as planned for a routine sensor sweep of Bexilite II, a planet in the Alakay system. Our mission is to seek out new sources of dilithium, and the early scans detected several lithium isotopes. It was all a promising start.

But Bexilite II is anything but a Class-M planet. It is a hell hole down there. The air is highly acidic and the surface temperature is like an oven. It took two days to modify a shuttle with thermal shielding and improve enough environmental suits. When Lieutenant Sandor noticed fluctuations in the lithium scans she insisted on going down to confirm the results. Against my better judgment, I allowed her to take a team down in the modified shuttle. My chief engineer was confident the shuttle would be fine, but I remained concerned we didn't have a second rescue shuttle ready, especially as we were having trouble getting a lock with the transporters.

Everything was fine until Sandor landed, and then the shuttle just vanished. We could find no answer for the disappearance, and scans revealed no wreckage. But we did discover a surge in chroniton particles, first on the planet, then in the quarters of Sandor and her landing team. They began to spread across the ship from there, in such concentrations, time is behaving strangely in the affected areas. We have seen it speed up and slow down, damaging the fabric of the ship and injuring crew members with the temporal strain.

I can't risk my crew by staying here, but I can't believe Sandor is gone. We need time to find them, but our own dilithium stores are highly sensitive to the chroniton particles and are melting away. I don't have much time, but we have no idea if leaving will solve the problems on the ship.

MIRACLE WORKER

REQUIREMENT: Engineering 5
You have a reputation of doing the impossible: repairs or modifications well in advance of expectations; getting offline systems up and running when most needed and so on. Whenever you use Engineering on an Extended Task, if you achieve a Breakthrough and roll at least one Effect on a Challenge Die, you achieve a second Breakthrough.

PROCEDURAL COMPLIANCE

REQUIREMENTS: Engineering 3+ and Conn 2+
You are well versed in established Starfleet engineering practices and guidelines. By spending 2 Momentum to *Create an Advantage* (obtaining the proper technical manuals and documentation prior to attempting a Task to work on a ship's system), you may reroll 1d20 during the next Engineering Task.

PAST THE REDLINE

REQUIREMENTS: Engineering 4+ and Daring 10+
Engineers understand that safety tolerances and operating margins are always designed into the acceptable performance range of equipment. While not recommended the equipment is usually capable of higher performance, if the consequences are risky. This Talent provides bonus Momentum for using a ship's System until the end of the scene. Select the System you wish to enhance, and the number of bonus Momentum to be provided. Attempt a **Daring + Engineering** Task with a Difficulty equal to the bonus Momentum selected.

If the you succeed, subsequent Tasks using that System automatically generate that amount of bonus Momentum. However, to represent the risks involved, the Task also increases its Complication Range by the same number as the Bonus Momentum provided. If a Complication is rolled, the System no longer provides bonus Momentum and the System suffers a number of Breaches equal to half the ship's Scale.

REPAIR TEAM LEADER

REQUIREMENTS: Engineering 3+ and Command 2+
You are trained to direct and lead damage repair parties during emergencies, giving them guidance and expert knowledge of the ships systems. If you succeed at the *Damage Control* Task (**Star Trek Adventures** core rulebook, p. 224) you may spend 3 Momentum (Repeatable) to also repair one Breach.

RIGHT TOOL FOR THE RIGHT JOB

REQUIREMENT: Engineering 3+
Engineers are trained to identify and use appropriate tools whenever they are working on the delicate components that make up complex ship systems. Whenever you acquire an engineering tool with an Opportunity Cost, the tool grants an Advantage if it did not do so originally, or increases the Advantage it provides by one step.

ROCKS INTO REPLICATORS

REQUIREMENTS: Engineering 4+ and Science 2+
Starfleet engineers are famed for being able to build or create nearly anything needed from the most basic of available components. Once per session, you may destroy any single piece of equipment to create any other piece of equipment of an equal or lower Opportunity Cost. This new piece of equipment has a Complication range increase of 2, with the Complication being a malfunction that renders it useless.

You should provide a reasonable explanation as to how a repurposed or cannibalized device could function and the Gamemaster has final say if there is any question about the "reasonableness" of the new device.

CHAPTER 04.00 ADVANCED TECHNOLOGY

8398734313234
902109124

04.10	ENGINEERING DEVICES	054
04.20	STARSHIP SYSTEMS	058
04.30	EXPERIMENTAL ENGINEERING	061

ADVANCED TECHNOLOGY
ENGINEERING DEVICES

"THIS IS GONNA BE LIKE PUTTIN' TOGETHER A BIG JIGSAW PUZZLE WHEN YOU DON'T EVEN KNOW WHAT THE PICTURE'S SUPPOSED TO BE."

— LIEUTENANT COMMANDER GEORDI LA FORGE

THE RIGHT TOOLS

Regardless of whether they are on a brand-new starship or attempting to repair an aging wreck that crashed more than a century ago and wasn't new back then, engineers require tools to perform their miracles. While the best Starfleet engineers are adaptable and can make do, having the correct tool for the job makes any job easier, faster, and safer for all concerned. The following are some of the more common and important tools that engineers regularly use.

COMMON ENGINEERING TOOLS

CUTTING TOOLS
The same technologies used in various devastating weapons can create equally powerful tools to cut and shape materials. Over the centuries of its existence, Starfleet has used a wide variety of cutting and drilling technologies. One common factor in all these devices is that any which are small enough to be easily carried and maneuvered can also be weapons, although none of them are as effective as purpose-built weaponry.

PLASMA TORCH
Plasma torches are somewhat bulky, roughly cylindrical devices. These powerful and useful general purpose cutting tools were in common use in the 22nd century and remain in use in the 24th century. Torches use exceptionally hot plasma to cut almost any material, including the advanced alloys used for starship hulls.

LASERS
Lasers are old and very reliable devices that are used in several different types of cutting devices. Laser drills can be found in both large varieties mounted on heavy equipment,

and as portable versions that can easily be carried in a standard backpack. Both the fixed and portable versions are most commonly used for mining and excavation. Laser torches are standard cutting tools that can be used for precise material crafting on materials including wood, metal, and stone. Laser welders are small handheld welders that can be used for all standard forms of metal welding.

MICRO-OPTIC DRILL (OPPORTUNITY 1)
This small and exceedingly precise hand tool can drill small holes through all common materials. The diameter of the holes it can create is variable, and it can even be set to drill microscopic holes.

PHASER DRILL (LARGE, OPPORTUNITY 1)
Phaser drills are bulky powerful tools used for cutting or blasting through large amounts of rock or other tough materials, including starship hulls. Phaser drills are relatively large devices mounted on 1.5-meter poles that anchor them. They are designed so that they can be used in groups to permit faster excavation or cutting.

ENGINEERING TRICORDER
This device is essentially a standard tricorder that has been modified to locate and diagnose problems in technological devices, particularly high energy devices like warp drives. It is most effective when analyzing Federation devices, and those of other known intelligent star-faring species, but it can provide a wealth of information about unknown alien technologies. However, this specialization and precision reduces the tricorder's range by half and reduces any information about living creatures. When closed an engineering tricorder appears superficially identical to a standard tricorder but, when open, it clearly possesses additional controls and readouts.

RULES
Compared to a standard tricorder, this device reduces the Difficulty of all attempts to locate energy sources, diagnose problems with technological devices by one, but has half

the range of a standard tricorder. It cannot be used to obtain detailed readings about living creatures or any medical problems they may have.

Engineering tricorders are standard issue for engineers, and do not have a cost.

OTHER TOOLS

FIELD DESTABILIZERS (OPPORTUNITY 1)

Force fields are used across the known Galaxy. When turning them off is not a convenient option, force fields can be disabled in two ways. The easiest method is to overload them by firing energy weapons like phasers or disruptors at them. Obviously, this method can damage people or devices protected by the force field, and a sufficiently powerful force field can resist all portable weapons. Field destabilizers are a safer and more powerful alternative. Typically used in pairs, they are set up on either side a doorway or other opening that is sealed by a force field the user wishes to take down.

Field destabilizers must be modulated to set up a destructive interference pattern that temporarily negates the force field. If the user does not already know the force field's resonant frequency, they must use a tricorder to find it. This process may require anywhere from a few seconds to several minutes. Once the user has determined the frequency, they input it into the field destabilizers which then temporarily negate the force field. Some advanced force fields, like those used by the Borg, use variable frequency modulation and thus are largely immune to the use of field destabilizers.

As long as both field destabilizers are not disturbed, the force field remains disabled. However, the field immediately reestablishes itself if either of the modulators is removed or deactivated. Standard portable field destabilizers are slender cylinders 25 centimeters tall and 1 centimeter in diameter, which include a tripod stand to keep them in place. These portable field destabilizers lack the power to deactivate the high-powered deflector shields used on starships.

HYPERSPANNER (STANDARD ISSUE FOR ENGINEERS, OPPORTUNITY 1 OTHERWISE)

Hyperspanners are somewhat heavy cylindrical devices roughly 30-40 centimeters long and several centimeters in diameter which function as a general-purpose engineering tool. They can be used to repair relays and circuits, alter and realign systems, and attach or unfasten screws, bolts, and other fasteners. They can be useful in a wide range of actions, ranging from exceedingly delicate functions like disarming the trigger mechanism of a complex bomb, to applications requiring significant power, like repairing an EPS conduit or a plasma injector.

MAGNETIC PROBE (OPPORTUNITY 1)

These devices are small cylinders approximately 20 centimeters long and slightly more than one centimeter in diameter. They are used to work with plasma flows and the magnetic fields that control them in EPS conduits. A magnetic probe can even be used to directly interact with the matter/antimatter flow in a starship's warp core. Before it is used, the probe's magnetic field must be adjusted to align with the magnetic flow of the field with which it is to interact.

Direct manipulation of an antimatter flow is extremely dangerous. Any serious mistake, like touching the probe on the side of the antimatter conduit can result in an uncontrolled explosion as the antimatter contacts both the probe and the user's arm. Used carefully, the probe's magnetic field prevents the device from physically contacting the antimatter flow. When used to work with antimatter rather than ordinary plasma, the user must reverse the probe's polarity. Failing to do this will also result in an enormous explosion!

HYPERSPANNER
MAGNETIC PROBE
SONIC DRIVER

12-0348

10-3893

09-3870

08-2229

6239-4760	5836	251872	23-305756	4673	84632
4936-2056	33839	220284	65-273396	21012	104585
5837-8200	28340	645640	29-285205	6203	650566

ENGINEERING ENSIGN SHRAN

COMMENDATION REQUEST, STARDATE 48315.3

After a cave-in at the Exo III archeological site, which trapped him and two other officers from the *U.S.S. Kagan*, Ensign Shran demonstrated himself to be a brilliant and resourceful young engineer. Lieutenant Martinez was injured, and her phaser destroyed in the cave-in, but Ensign Shran modified a combadge and a tricorder to emit a series of tightly focused phaser pulses to drill a hole in the planet's surface. He then used a combadge and the remaining tricorder to focus and amplify the signal from the final combadge so that it could reach orbit through this hole. As a result of this action, Ensign Shran, and Lieutenants Martinez and Cho were all rescued before the second seismic event, which collapsed the small cavern where these three young officers had been trapped.

SONIC DRIVER (OPPORTUNITY 1)

This small, lightweight hand tool can open access panels and to remove or replace fasteners of all types swiftly and without the necessity of using any manual force. In effect, it is a general-purpose tool for either attaching or removing screws, bolts, and other fasteners far more rapidly and easily than would be possible using unpowered tools. A hyperspanner can also perform all these functions, but a sonic driver is small enough to fit easily into a pocket or equipment pouch.

TRANSPORT INHIBITOR (OPPORTUNITY 1)

These devices are the opposite of pattern enhancers (*Star Trek Adventures* core rulebook p. 199). They prevent transporters from being used to materialize or dematerialize people or objects within a specific area. Inhibitors emit a variable energy field which prevents a transporter from obtaining a pattern lock on the protected area and everything inside it. They can be adjusted to alter the size and shape of this protected area, with the maximum protected area for one transporter inhibitor being a 10m circle around the device.

Multiple transporter inhibitors can be used to protect a larger region from transporter activity. When arranged correctly, a relatively small number of transporter inhibitors can be used to screen an area of up to several hundred meters on a side. The destruction or deactivation of a few inhibitors produces gaps in the protection and, if too many are destroyed, most of the area ceases to be protected. Transport inhibitors are relatively large devices consisting of a two-meter cylinder topped by a wide, flat emitter.

JURY-RIGGED DEVICES

Sometimes engineers don't possess the correct tools for the job, or perhaps they have an excellent selection of tools, but lack crucial parts required to repair or construct a device and the nearest replicator is dozens of kilometers or light-years away. Fortunately, the skilled engineers who created Starfleet devices were aware that such situations would occur, and they did their best to provide alternatives.

Starfleet engineers and technicians understand that all Starfleet devices are overdesigned. In addition to permitting long-term use under sub-optimal conditions and easy repairs, almost all standard Starfleet devices are designed with compatible parts. While causing some devices to be slightly larger than needed, this design choice has two advantages. Firstly, different devices can be used to repair one another. Combadge components, for example, can be used to repair a phaser or a tricorder. Secondly, with tools, time, and a clear understanding of Federation technology, individuals can alter the functions of various Starfleet devices, using them to substitute for one another to a limited degree. For example, a combadge could be jury-rigged to provide a short term personal shield or a one-shot phaser, while a phaser could be repurposed to send out a subspace distress call.

However, several factors must be kept in mind when such modifications are attempted. The first is that all such changes render a device useless for its original purpose. Also, improvised devices never function as well as one built to perform the designed function. Finally, nothing can increase the amount of power available in a device's battery. A combadge can only provide a personal shield that only operates for a few seconds or a single medium stun phaser bolt; a phaser's much larger power cell could operate a subspace beacon for several days.

RULES ADVICE

Obtaining replacement parts from unrelated devices, such as using a phaser power cell to power a tricorder is relatively straightforward. This is typically a Difficulty 1 Task but increase this Difficulty by +1 or even +2 if the character lacks proper tools. In contrast, jury-rigging a combadge into a personal forcefield or a tricorder into a one-shot phaser should never be easy. The minimum Difficulty should never be less than 2 and is often 3. A lack of proper tools increases this Difficulty by +1 or even +2.

As with all Engineering Tasks, if the character lacks any remotely useful tools then the task is likely to be impossible.

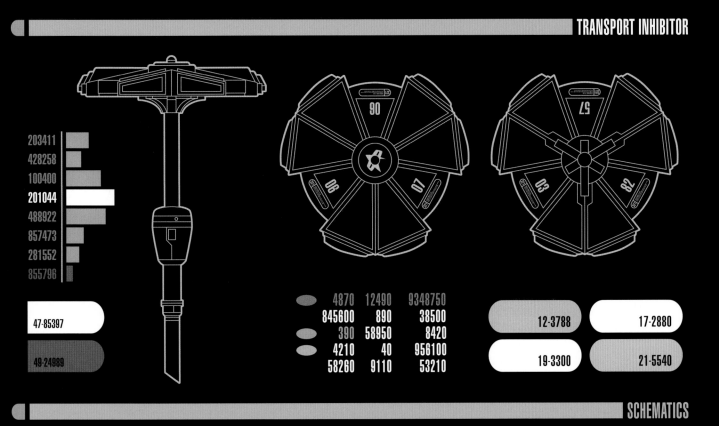

ADVANCED TECHNOLOGY
STARSHIP SYSTEMS

"I'VE GIV'N HER ALL SHE'S GOT CAPTAIN, AN' I CANNAE GIVE HER NO MORE."

— LT. COMMANDER MONTGOMERY SCOTT

DESIGN FLEXIBILITY

Federation starships are overbuilt and contain a large degree of flexibility. One of the most notable aspects of this design philosophy is in the use of plasma and EPS (electro-plasma system) conduits that transfer power throughout a starship. These conduits allow engineers to swiftly transfer large amounts of power where it is needed, including into systems which do not normally require or use vast amounts of energy. This flexibility, combined with the ability to reconfigure ship systems on the fly, and that many systems are designed to survive temporary overloads has enabled daring engineers to save ships by routing around damage to power to critical systems, or to temporarily rework a system to perform well beyond its normal operating parameters for a short time.

STARSHIP TECHNOLOGY

ARTIFICIAL GRAVITY & INERTIAL COMPENSATORS

The use of artificial gravity on starships allows the crew to be healthier, comfortable and effective. The closely related inertial dampers are vitally necessary for survival because they greatly reduce the effects of acceleration and deceleration. Gravity generators are installed in the duranium gravity plating and the inertial dampers are linked to them. Both systems are part of a starship's gravimetric generation and inertial damping subsystem. The inertial dampers are installed alongside the structure integrity field and maintain their field throughout the entire vessel by using multiple redundant generators. Whenever a starship performs extensive maneuvers, such as in battle, inertial dampers are needed but they are most important in the acceleration necessary before entering warp drive and deceleration immediately after leaving warp as a ship accelerates up to or down from near light speed. An inertial damper failure at that time is almost always fatal to the entire crew as they are suddenly subjected to many hundred times Earth's gravity.

Gravity generators and gravity plating can be adjusted. This is done regularly in shuttlebays to prevent shuttles from encountering sharp gravity gradients, but it can also be done to permit low-gravity sports in starship recreation areas, to provide for aliens from low or high gravity worlds, to alter local gravity in a section of the hull to either impede intruders or assist with repairs by increasing crew mobility. An engineer with control of a starship's gravity and inertial damping could adjust it to render anyone helpless (or kill them) in part of the ship, while leaving the rest of the ship entirely unaffected.

CONTAINMENT FIELDS & EMERGENCY FORCE FIELDS

Most modern starships are fitted with force fields throughout their internal structure. These force field emitters can be found every few meters along corridors, at locations designed to act as force field bulkheads, at all major corridor junctions, and in every section of the ship with critical or potentially dangerous equipment.

While these fields are normally used to seal hull breaches, contain damaged systems that are emitting dangerous energies, and to isolate contagious occupants or hostile intruders, they can be adapted to other purposes. By activating the force field emitters in a corridor in sequence, they can isolate sections of the ship, allowing an engineer to move through the ship relatively safety from intruders or any other threat.

While these force fields most often form walls, cylinders, or on occasions domes, they can be set to produce a variety of shapes. A starship's internal force field emitters can provide protection and also create simple but strong formattable structures. They can be used to bridge damaged sections of the ship or, in an emergency, to provide access to areas that are otherwise cut off. Because force fields leave serious, but not life-threatening, burns when their formation intersects a living body they can function as limited weapons if their activation is carefully timed.

Serious force field malfunctions, or having their operations suborned by hostile sentients, can be a serious threat, and individuals can end up isolated from one another on different sides of a field, or trapped. Because transporters cannot normally function through force fields, their use can also isolate areas of the ship from both direct physical and transporter access.

REPLICATORS

Derived from transporter technology, replicators are the basis for the Federation's economy. Replicators dematerialize matter and rematerialize it in a variety of organized forms, including as food and drink, clothing, spare parts, and materials made of almost all substances except a few items that cannot be replicated, like latinum. Some Humans claim that they can taste the difference between natural and replicated food and drink. More importantly, like transporters, replicators use large amounts of energy. Starships that are running short of energy may need to ration replicator use to avoid power shortages.

However, replicators cannot recreate anything and everything: materials that are too complex cannot be replicated, but this limitation primarily applies to complex biological materials like some medicines. Federation replicators cannot create advanced multicellular lifeforms, but other civilizations have managed to do so. Replicating people and animals is, therefore, theoretically possible.

There are several common types of replicators. Standard replicators are small devices typically found in replimats, crew quarters, and starship replicating centers. They can produce food, drink, clothing, and various small items like plates, decorations, or small weapons. Industrial replicators can produce larger items, and can replicate a wider variety of materials, including exotic substances like the explosive trilithium and even protomatter. Finally, genetronic replicators, developed by Dr. Toby Russell in 2368, are an experimental technology that can produce custom tissues and organs using the patient's genetic information. This device could revolutionize transplantation surgery but is currently a somewhat unreliable prototype.

Like transporters, Federation replicators possess biofilters to prevent the creation of dangerous diseases. They are prohibited from creating various toxins without a command override or similar authorization, just as they also prevent unauthorized creation of Starfleet uniforms, powerful weapons, and dangerous substances. However, they are both exceedingly powerful devices and nearly ubiquitous, so engineers use them for a wide variety of unintended purposes. Realigning a replicator's matter energy conversion matrix can turn it into a miniature short range transporter, but it can only transport objects of a size that it can replicate, and a replicator-transporter is not safe to transport living creatures.

Hacking a replicator's biofilter or the limitation circuits can allow clever engineers to triumph in desperate circumstances by creating custom-made diseases, intoxicants, or toxins in replicated items, including food. Similar efforts can allow a replicator to create a phaser or similar weapons. A well-maintained industrial replicator and a reliable supply of both

energy and matter allows an engineer to do anything from completely rebuilding almost any badly damaged starship, to providing a lower-technology colony with everything it requires to substantially advance its technology.

TRANSPORTERS

While among the most complex systems on a starship, basic transporters are relatively straightforward. The operator first locks onto the target; this can be an individual to be beamed up, or the beaming destination. The individual or individuals being transported are scanned using the molecular imaging scanner, and the Heisenberg compensators that are part of this system eliminate quantum effect problems. As the scan ends an individual is dematerialized and transformed into a matter stream. As the transport lock is checked a final time the matter stream is briefly stored in the pattern buffer, and then beamed through subspace to its destination. The transporter's annular confinement beam keeps the matter stream stable until the matter stream rematerializes at the destination, where the scanner's data is used to precisely reconstruct the individual.

Like all Starfleet systems, transporters can be used well beyond their designed operational parameters. For example, the pattern buffer is intended to store a dematerialized matter stream for up to seven minutes to ensure that the beaming minimizes relative motion between the subject and their destination. It is possible to extend the time a matter stream can remain in a pattern buffer before it begins to seriously degrade. The current record is 75 years, achieved when Captain Montgomery Scott successfully stored himself in a transporter's pattern buffer by disabling the rematerialization circuits and placing the transporter in a continuous diagnostic cycle. This amazing feat was only partly successful: Captain Scott went into the pattern buffer with another person, but only he survived.

There is a problem of transporting through raised shields and force fields, but there are some ways around this difficulty. Some starships use powerful sensor systems that require periodic "windows" in their shields to operate at peak efficiency. Knowledge of these sensor windows can

REPLICATOR ETHICS

Obviously, allowing any pre-warp civilization access to a replicator is a serious violation of the Prime Directive. However, the ethical position is less clear for early warp-capable civilizations. While not expressly forbidden, giving a less advanced civilization access to even a single replicator can drastically transform it, both technologically and socially. While there may be good reasons for granting replicator access, any Starfleet personnel who do so should be prepared to justify their actions to their superiors.

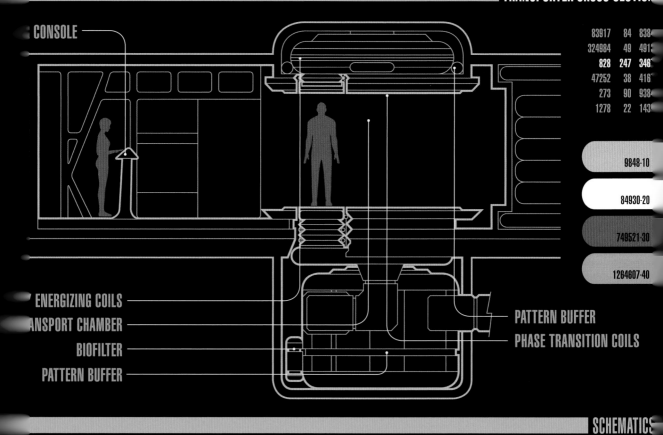

CONSOLE

ENERGIZING COILS
TRANSPORT CHAMBER
BIOFILTER
PATTERN BUFFER

PATTERN BUFFER
PHASE TRANSITION COILS

83917 84 838
324984 49 491
828 247 346
47252 38 416
273 90 938
1278 22 143

9848-10
84930-20
749521-30
1264607-40

allow transport though the shields, but only if the engineer operating the transporter has a precise knowledge of the other target's sensors and shields.

Transporter biofilters remove all known diseases and parasites from an individual's pattern but cannot handle unknown threats. Once a disease or parasite has been identified, though, any transporter can be reconfigured to filter it out. In addition, while risky enough to be considered only in an emergency, intraship beaming allows Starfleet personnel to move from one section of a starship to another in seconds, including rematerializing in exceedingly cramped spaces. The subject must crouch in an appropriate posture to fit where they are going and be willing to risk serious consequences if the transport is not perfect.

Another useful transporter function is the weapons-deactivation program. This can be set to render weapons in the transporter's database useless after they have been transported, allowing someone to transport armed invaders or mutineers to a secure cell, and then prevent them using their weapons after they arrive. While tricky and requiring significant skill, maintaining a continuous transporter lock on an individual or an entire away team allows a starship to beam an away team up in less than a second, rather than the minute or two beaming normally requires.

Of course, these tricks are part of the normal transporter operation. By making use of the vast store of information available on transporter problems, a skilled engineer could also alter someone's biological age in either direction, or fully restore a victim of a serious accident or injury. An engineer might even be able to bring someone who recently died back to life. Through the initiation of multiple annular confinement beams in one transport, it is even possible to exactly duplicate individuals, perhaps multiple times, potentially enabling the creation of dozens of initially identical individuals.

All these options could have serious consequences, including memory loss, serious personality changes, dangerous insanity, or death. Some engineers are convinced that transporters could be used to fully rejuvenate the elderly with no loss of memory or experience but, like all tests involving intelligent subjects, there are important ethical considerations, not to mention the problem of obtaining approval from Starfleet for any such test.

WARP DRIVE
This advanced technology binds the Federation together as a political unit. The independent creation of warp drive is also the mark of an interstellar civilization that can be openly contacted by the Federation. The heart of a starship's warp drive is the warp core or matter/antimatter reaction chamber, where deuterium and anti-deuterium react, releasing vast

quantities of energy. Dilithium crystals moderate this reaction, preventing an explosion. Instead an electro-plasma is created that powers a starship's warp engines and provides energy for most of a starship's systems.

Plasma is directed to its destinations through plasma conduits, which are part of the starship's EPS (electro-plasma system). These conduits use powerful magnets to contain and direct the plasma to various destinations. The highest energy plasma is directed into the starship's warp nacelles where it energizes the warp coils, creating the subspace displacement field that allows the starship to travel faster than light.

Control of a starship's plasma conduits allows an engineer to direct energy to or away from various systems, which can be used to provide the excess energy needed to temporarily overdrive a system, or to shut off a system so that any hostiles aboard a starship cannot use it. If an engineer prevents the EPS from delivering plasma to weapons systems or shields, the starship cannot use either.

The most dangerous portion of the entire system is the warp core. Powerful magnetic fields keep the antimatter contained before and during its entry into the warp core, and failure of these fields can result in a warp core breach that swiftly transforms a starship into a world-destroying bomb. While rare, the most common causes for a warp core breach are coolant leaks severe enough to damage the magnetic containment system, severe power surges, impurities in the deuterium or antideuterium, high levels of antineutrinos, and physical damage to the magnetic containment system.

Although emergency magnetic fields can keep a damaged warp core stable for a short period of time, only prompt action by an engineer can restore warp core stability. If this proves impossible, an engineer must eject the warp core, which leaves the starship intact but unable to use the warp drive until a new warp core can be assembled. If the warp core cannot be ejected, the captain must either separate its primary hull from the engineering hull and the warp core (if such separation is possible) or order the crew to abandon ship.

There are reasons why an engineer might want to either induce a warp core breach or eject a starship's warp core. Inducing or simulating an imminent warp core breach can cause mutineers or invaders to swiftly abandon a starship. While ejecting a warp core is a drastic step, the resulting explosion can sometimes heal subspace tears. Finally, the force of such a massive blast can either destroy almost any threat or push the starship away from a danger it cannot otherwise avoid.

CHAPTER 04.30

ADVANCED TECHNOLOGY
EXPERIMENTAL ENGINEERING

THE M-5 MULTITRONIC UNIT & FEDERATION ARTIFICIAL INTELLIGENCE

The first true artificial intelligence created in the Federation was the M-5 multitronic unit constructed by Dr. Richard Daystrom in 2268. Daystrom developed multitronic circuitry specifically for this computer and planned to replace the standard duotronic circuits which he had developed two decades earlier. Because Daystrom was seeking to construct a computer that could think like a human, but with a superior intellect, he used his recorded human memory engrams as a model for the computer's artificial mind. While the M-5 computer was brilliant, and could easily control

THE CUTTING EDGE

Engineers are not content only to repair or improve the efficiency of existing systems. Some work to create entirely new devices that significantly advance Federation technology.

an entire starship with only minimal human assistance, it ultimately proved to be unstable. The use of human memory engrams produced human emotions and drives that it made it prone to irrational emotional outbursts. M5 also exhibited a willingness to kill humans that threatened it or

even seemed a threat, but it eventually shut down when confronted with the deeply immoral nature of its actions. Although exceptionally advanced and to some degree conscious and self-aware, the M-5 computer was a marvel but not entirely sane.

The next major step in the creation of artificial intelligence was Dr. Noonien Soong's development of androids in the first few decades of the 24th Century. All these androids possessed advanced positronic brains whose artificial neural networks mimicked human brains. Solving the problem of the electron resistance across the neural filaments was one of the many challenges involved in creating stable positronic brains. While androids have the potential to make artificial intelligence commonplace in the Federation, the now deceased Dr. Soong was the only researcher who was able to create stable positronic brains, and three of the seven he created failed utterly. As a result, while creating, repairing, and modifying android bodies can be accomplished by any skilled engineer, creating or even duplicating a stable positronic brain is an exceedingly difficult challenge that can be attempted only by the finest engineers. In addition to the risks of the brain's neural net suffering a cascade failure if the android encounters sufficient mental or emotional stress, the ethical and legal ramifications are far from trivial. Federation law now recognizes one Soong-type android, Lieutenant Commander Data, as being legally a person. As a result, any engineer who creates an android would probably be

creating a new person and not merely a machine. The legal status of a sentient computer like the M-5 is far less clear.

PHASING CLOAK

COST: OPPORTUNITY 2, ESCALATION 2
The Federation captured a Romulan cloaking device in 2268. Starfleet engineers and scientists worked for many years to find its weaknesses, and also to duplicate and improve upon it. However, the 2311 Treaty of Algeron between the Federation and the Romulan Star Empire strictly prohibited the Federation from developing or using cloaking technology.

This prohibition did not stop the Federation clandestinely researching prototypes of several types of cloaking devices. The most impressive, a phasing cloak, was first tested on the *U.S.S. Pegasus* in 2358, under the command of Captain Erik Pressman. It concealed the vessel from sensors and vision, and rendered the vessel out of phase with the physical universe, allowing it pass through normal matter easily and unharmed. Unfortunately, in its first test, the cloak overloaded the ship's plasma relays and failed just as the ship was passing through an asteroid, resulting in the starship melding with part of the asteroid. In 2368, an *Enterprise* away team used both Lieutenant Commander Data's built-in phase discriminator, and a tricorder with a custom-made phase discriminator installed, to render themselves 0.004 percent out of phase with the physical universe. This made them invisible, but able to perceive the alien Devidians, who are naturally out of phase.

While difficult to maintain for an entire starship, phasing technology offers excellent opportunities to make valuable discoveries for adventurous engineers. However, rendering an object sufficiently out of phase to become invisible is considerably easier than causing the object to become sufficiently out of phase to safely interpenetrate other matter. This technology is considered to violate the Treaty of Algeron.

In addition to solving the problem of instability in large phase shifts, if an engineer could find some way to permit people or starships to go sufficiently out of phase to pass through matter without becoming invisible, such technology would not violate the Treaty of Algeron. A device along these lines could allow individuals to pass through walls and perhaps even starships to freely move through planets, as well as offering an impressive defense against most attacks. The first step in creating such a device would be to build or adapt a phase discriminator that could shift something sufficiently out of phase to allow it to pass through solid matter, while also solving the instability problems that the phased cloak on the *U.S.S. Pegasus* suffered from. The next problem is finding a way for a phased person or object to remain visible.

SOLITON WAVE GENERATOR

In 2368, Dr. Ja'Dar of Bilana III tested an alternative to conventional warp drive, the soliton wave generator. This wave was generated on Bilana III by a series of 23 field coils. This soliton wave traveled at warp speeds, and could push a small ship along with it. For Ja'Dar's test, the soliton wave was direct at Lemma II three light years away, where an associated base would generate a particle scattering field to dissipate the soliton wave, returning the small ship to normal space. The only energy used in the procedure would be the brief operation of the field coils at the point of departure and the equally short operation of the particle scattering field generator at the destination. If perfected, this method of transport would allow simple low-cost vessels to carry passengers and cargo between worlds equipped with paired soliton wave and particle scattering field generators, doing away with the need for most conventional starship travel between such worlds.

Unfortunately, the soliton wave proved to be unstable. It destroyed the ship and rapidly increased in both warp factor and energy well beyond what the Lemma II base could dissipate. If the Enterprise had not destroyed the wave with a photon torpedo burst, the wave would have destroyed the Lemma II colony and might have destroyed the entire planet. This increasing energy occurred after the wave was generated and the field coils were turned off.

The test was a serious failure, and future experiments will need to be done with far greater care, but the theory remains sound. A team of careful and dedicated engineers could theoretically create a working version of this technology. This would revolutionize passenger and cargo transport throughout the Federation. However, one limitation of a functional soliton wave transport system is that the likely velocity would be between warp 2 and warp 4: travel to a nearby star would require several weeks unless the warp factor could be increased. However, some passengers might prefer this method of travel, and its ease of use would make it ideal for interstellar cargo transport.

Making this system functional would involve increasing the stability of the soliton wave and making certain that the field no longer increased in energy after it was generated. Alternatively, a sufficiently desperate engineer could attempt to deliberately enhance this instability and energy increase, creating a devastatingly effective planetary defense system. Once fired it could damage or destroy an entire attacking fleet and displace any surviving ships to some point light years away.

- **Soliton Wave Damage:** (Energy, Range Long, 12▲ Vicious 1, Devastating, High-Yield)

SYNAPTIC SCANNING TECHNIQUE

COST: OPPORTUNITY 2

One of the by-products of artificial intelligence research is the attempt by some scientists and engineers to transfer human minds into android bodies, or perhaps even into computers. The android duplicating machine on Exo III — see the **Star Trek Adventures** core rulebook (p. 333-334) — proved that doing so is possible, although those transfers were imperfect. There have been several other attempts to create devices that accomplish this goal. The most well documented is the mind transference technique developed by Dr. Ira Graves in his attempt to transfer his consciousness into the android Lieutenant Commander Data in 2365. Because Dr. Graves later transferred all his knowledge into the Enterprise's computers, detailed information about his technique is available to any engineer who wishes to duplicate them.

Although the details are less well known, Dr. Graves' student Dr. Noonian Soong developed what he called a synaptic scanning technique, which he used to scan the mind of geologist Juliana Tainer and transfer it into an android body before her death. Although this transference seems to have been entirely successful, part of the reason may have been that Dr. Tainer was entirely unaware that she had an android body. This android body was designed to both fool ordinary medical scans and appear to be physically human in all ways, including simulating aging. The moral and ethical questions posed by these techniques are immense, especially since it is now possible for human engineers to construct androids that are almost impossible to distinguish from humans using any non-invasive means.

REPORT TO THE DAYSTROM INSTITUTE

STARDATE 41986.1

The first in-flight test of the M11 freighter control unit was what I can best describe as a dubious success. The unit successfully piloted the freighter from Earth to Alpha Centauri, and did so cheerfully and in good spirits. However, while the cargo suffered no damage, I am concerned that M11 used its drones to arrange the cargo into elaborate sculptures. I am even more troubled that on arrival it attempted to negotiate a better price for the cargo. I don't know if we're seeing signs of building instability, or simply an overly active imagination combined with a strong desire to succeed at its missions. Regardless, in my opinion the M11 isn't remotely ready for commercial use.

— Dr. Kathryn Ngomo

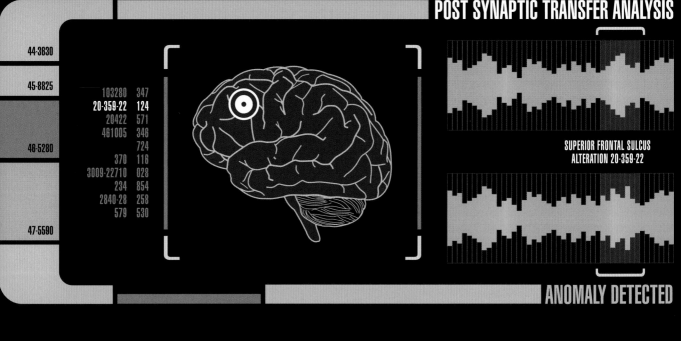

44-3630

45-8825

46-5280

47-5590

103280   347
20-359-22   124
20422   571
461005   346
724
370   116
3009-22710   028
234   854
2840-28   258
579   530

SUPERIOR FRONTAL SULCUS
ALTERATION 20-359-22

ANOMALY DETECTED

In addition, ensuring that the transfer is complete and does not degrade the subject's mind is difficult, as is constructing a stable positronic brain for the android. Although Dr. Noonian Soong managed both tasks, others were less successful. One key aspect of producing a successful transfer is making certain that the scanned personality is sufficiently intact and undamaged that it does not suffer from ethical degradation, and the replacement of morality with callous utilitarianism that both the Exo III transfer process and Ira Graves' process suffered from.

In addition, all known techniques for synaptic transfer and most similar techniques of mental transference result in the death of the subject being scanned, so there is no room for error in this procedure. Any engineer attempting to replicate or advance this work must contend with difficult problems of morality and engineering. Any such attempts would only be permitted with terminally ill volunteers and, even then, obtaining permission for these experiments from a Starfleet ethics board would not be easy. Starfleet would expect clear proof that the experiment would not, and could not, have monstrous results.

TRANSWARP DRIVE

Modern warp drive is exceptionally fast, allowing starships to journey to nearby stars in no more than a few days. However, distant stars can still require weeks of travel to reach, and visiting another quadrant requires decades at maximum warp. Starfleet engineers are therefore continually searching for speedier methods of travel. Transwarp drive has proven to be the most promising technology, but also the most elusive.

The first attempt at creating a transwarp drive was the construction of the *U.S.S. Excelsior* in 2285. However, continuing problems with that ship's transwarp drive resulted in it eventually being refitted with conventional warp drive.

After 2371, the discovery of the Borg transwarp conduits, and the transwarp coils used on many Borg vessels, revolutionized work on transwarp technologies. Borg transwarp coils allow starships to travel 20,000 light years in a few days, making it hundreds of times faster than vessels capable of traveling at Warp 9.99. In addition, experiences with other highly advanced species indicate that even faster drives are possible.

After 2371, Starfleet vessels can be adapted to use Borg transwarp corridors and transwarp coil components, but duplicating either technology has proven impossible. So far, no engineer has managed to keep a transwarp coil working for more than a few days. In addition, maintaining a Federation vessel at transwarp speeds requires both great care and extensive maintenance afterwards. Any engineer who could stabilize a captured Borg transwarp coil so that both it, and the ship carrying it, could survive prolonged use would greatly advance Starfleet warp technology and mobility. Once this has been accomplished, duplicating a Borg transwarp coil is the next step to providing Starfleet with transwarp technology, but this device is significantly in advance of current Federation technology.

Any engineer attempting this feat must choose between either trying to precisely duplicate a technology they do not fully understand, or reverse engineering the transwarp coil's function so that it is within the limits of Federation technology. The second option will be far easier to mass produce, but the resulting device will almost certainly be slower, larger, less energy efficient, and possibly less reliable than a Borg transwarp coil.

USING THE
OPERATIONS DIVISION

492850926598
121329584960120

05.10   SECURITY DEPARTMENT STORYLINES   066

05.20   ENGINEERING DEPARTMENT STORYLINES   075

USING THE OPERATIONS DIVISION
SECURITY DEPARTMENT STORYLINES

"PHASERS READY. PHOTON TORPEDOES STANDING BY. LOCKING ON TARGET."

— LIEUTENANT WORF

BEYOND THE FINAL FRONTIER

The **Star Trek Adventures** core rulebook (p. 298) offered a means of resolving encounters via a color-coded system of plot components:

- **Red plot components** focus on diplomacy, first contact, legal drama, politics, and anything of a spiritual theme that doesn't fit within a science plot.

- **Gold plot components** emphasize personal or ship combat, physical activities, espionage, and other action-oriented themes.

- **Blue plot components** involve science, medicine, engineering, technology, and tactical situations that fit outside the criteria for gold components.

Chapter 5 of the Command Division supplemental rulebook expanded on this concept by providing red, gold, and blue plot components geared towards command division characters. Following is a similar offering of plot components geared towards security department characters.

RED PLOT COMPONENTS

Red plot components for security officers usually entail safeguarding parties involved in diplomatic exchanges, be they the officer's fellow crewmen or members of a third party. Security officers might also be called upon to employ their investigative skills to determine if any wrongdoing is at work by any of the interested parties or if someone intends to sabotage negotiations for their selfish ends.

Use this random table to generate a quick red plot component to incorporate into your mission or generate a story idea for your security Player Characters.

GENERATING RED PLOT COMPONENTS

D20 ROLL	RED PLOT COMPONENT
1	Conspiracy
2–6	Diplomacy
7–11	First Contact
12–14	Political
15–17	Show the Flag
18–19	Spiritual
20	Starfleet JAG

CONSPIRACIES

A security officer will often find their investigative acumen tested in the case of conspiracy scenarios, as the investigation of a crime, as well as determining who amongst a group is either trustworthy or a conspirator, would fall within the security department's purview. Security officers are often the first to encounter a conspiracy, as the investigation of a catastrophic event could lead to the discovery that the event was the work of a plan orchestrated by a number of key individuals, either those of an outside power, within the Federation, or a combination of the two.

Security officers are also prime candidates for recruitment into conspiracies, as their combat prowess makes them ideal to enforce the will of the conspiracy. Gamemasters could present such a scenario as a challenge to security Player Characters; though a Player Character turning against his crew for the sake of what the conspiracy describes as a greater good is unlikely, a Gamemaster could potentially provide narrative incentive via the character's Values that would tempt them towards making a potentially unwise choice.

DIPLOMACY

As stated above, a security officer will often find themselves seeing to the safety of those involved in complex negotiations over an important issue such as the control of territory, the mobilization of military force, or, as the Federation is often called to mediate, terms of peace between two belligerent powers. Diplomatic missions require a security presence not only to safeguard the away team but to oversee security for the negotiations taking place and to prevent elements within the parties involved with a vested interest in the negotiations failing from taking any form of subversive or hostile action.

Security officers assigned to diplomatic missions per away team security protocols are required to coordinate with the law enforcement authorities of the parties involved, even if the security officer and the native law enforcement officials are in total disagreement over how to best secure the negotiations.

FIRST CONTACT

A crew's security department is arguably an essential part of any first contact situation, as maintaining the safety of their crew during something as completely unknown and unpredictable a scenario as meeting with a culture either largely or totally unknown is customarily paramount. Security officers will often be placed on away teams assigned to first contact missions and are often assigned, along with science officers of a sociological discipline, to review the customs and laws of a newly discovered culture to ensure that no laws are inadvertently broken by any away team member that would leave them at the mercy of the culture's judicial system.

POLITICAL

Security officers could be called to intervene in a variety of political scenarios. A security officer might find themselves as the designated bodyguard for a foreign dignitary en route to defuse a political crisis within his culture of origin or between his culture and another. Such an assignment could prove a wellspring for narrative drama; perhaps the dignitary is socially unpleasant or, worse, originate from a

culture with a longstanding feud with that of the officer's. A security officer may also be asked to employ their tactical and investigative expertise to analyze a tragic event that ignited tensions between two rival factions or to determine potential outcomes if a simmering distrust were to explode into a shooting war.

SHOW THE FLAG

During missions wherein a crew is dispatched to establish Federation authority of a member world or another culture that is dismissive of the Federation, a security officer could easily find themselves at the forefront of keeping the peace and applying Federation law, and, if peaceful means of defusing the situation fail, through the use of appropriate force.

SPIRITUAL

Spiritual experiences are command-style plot components because they don't really fit anywhere else. The warrior-style spiritualism of the Klingons is practiced quite devoutly by Lt. Worf throughout his time in Starfleet - and any cultural significance of the death of a security officer may be pertinent to the stories you tell.

STARFLEET JAG

Though the Judge Advocate General's office typically employ its own dedicated investigative officers, JAG officers assigned to frontier colonies or outposts or those simply short-staffed may find cause to recruit a security Player Character to lead an investigation into a case of potential misconduct on the part of another Starfleet officer. The JAG may also target a security officer for investigation themselves following a combat situation that went awry to determine if the officer under scrutiny exercised good judgment while under fire.

BLUE PLOT COMPONENTS

Blue plot components focus primarily on science and technology. Security officers have at the minimum a basic level of remedial cross-training in sciences and engineering,

CRIME AND THE PRIME DIRECTIVE

Part of the Prime Directive's non-interference doctrine states that the laws of unaligned worlds are to be respected and followed, even if a Starfleet representative is accused or even convicted of a crime. Starfleet may intervene in a criminal investigation on an unaligned world only if the world's government requests their assistance or agrees to a request by Starfleet personnel to involve themselves.

Any Starfleet personnel accused of a crime are subject to the laws of that world, up to and including conviction and sentencing, and the Prime Directive forbids Starfleet personnel from interfering in the legal process in any manner that violates the planet's laws. Essentially, if a Starfleet officer is convicted of a crime and sentenced for punishment, even if the sentence is long-term imprisonment or execution, Starfleet can legally do nothing save for petitioning the Federation to seek the officer's release through diplomatic means or, if the officer was falsely accused, present evidence that the officer is innocent or identify the true perpetrator.

and some security officers supplement their training in subjects that would aid in their careers in security, such as tactical systems engineering and medical training.

Use this random table to generate a quick blue plot component to incorporate into your mission or generate a story idea for your security Player Characters.

D20 ROLL	BLUE PLOT COMPONENT
1–5	Deep Space Exploration
6–7	Evacuation
8–9	Medical Issue
10–14	Near Space Exploration
15–17	Planetary Exploration
18–20	Research

EPISODES FOCUSED ON SECURITY CHALLENGES

"THE EXPANSE" (ENTERPRISE)

Enterprise-NX returns to Earth to discover seven million people were killed in an attack orchestrated by the Xindi; with the ship and crew upgraded for combat, *Enterprise* travels to the Delphic Expanse to stop the Xindi from launching another attack.

"BALANCE OF TERROR" (THE ORIGINAL SERIES)

After multiple Neutral Zone outposts are destroyed by a Romulan bird-of-prey, the first encountered in over a century, the *Enterprise*, in the face of the ship's superior firepower and cloaking technology, pursues the hostile craft.

"THE HUNTED" (THE NEXT GENERATION)

While evaluating Angosia III for Federation membership, the *Enterprise-D* crew encounter a genetically enhanced Angosian soldier whose physical and strategic abilities stymie attempts to contain him.

"NECESSARY EVIL" (DEEP SPACE NINE)

Odo returns to an unsolved murder case from the days of the Cardassian occupation (his first as Deep Space 9's constable) when an attack on Quark brings new evidence to light.

"MESSAGE IN A BOTTLE" (VOYAGER)

Tuvok investigates a murder on the homeworld of the Baneans when Tom Paris is falsely convicted of the crime and sentenced to implantation of a regularly recurring memory of the murder.

DEEP SPACE EXPLORATION

The exploration of uncharted is potentially fraught with unseen hazards, requiring a security officer to remain at a high level of vigilance. In tandem with a ship's science officer, a security officer maintains a watchful eye for spatial phenomena that may pose a threat to their ship and crew. Should a calamity befall the ship due to an encounter with a previously unknown cosmic phenomenon, the security officer may supplement the work of the ship's engineering department to develop a defense against further adverse effects resulting from proximity with the phenomenon.

EVACUATION

Evacuating a ship, outpost, or world is often a chaotic venture, and a security officer may be placed in charge of making sure that evacuees are transported safely and without incident. If the security officer's ship finds itself having to house evacuees for an extended period, keeping order amongst the evacuee population during their time on the ship would fall under the security officer's duties. If the reason for the evacuation of the inhabitants' home was due to an attack by a hostile force, the chaos of the endeavor may be compounded by the hostile force returning to finish what they started, which may place the security officer's ship in their crosshairs.

MEDICAL ISSUE

A planetary or outpost-scale medical crisis poses a unique challenge to a security officer, as they must not only contend with enforcing quarantines, but maintaining order among both the afflicted and unafflicted. Those that have become

AWAY TEAMS IN THE ENTERPRISE AND ORIGINAL SERIES ERAS

In the earlier eras of play, away teams, or "landing parties" as they were referred to in the Original Series era, were conducted in much the same way as those of the Next Generation era with a few key exceptions. In addition to the change in terminology, Starfleet in the 22nd and 23rd centuries was more lenient on the matter of a starship's captain leading landing parties. Whereas 24th century Starfleet

protocol established that away teams should be led by the ship's executive officer with the second officer as the team's second-in-command, 22nd and 23rd century landing parties were often led by the ship's captain, with the executive officer as the team's second-in-command and temporary command of the ship assigned to the second officer.

STARFLEET REGULATIONS

AWAY TEAM SECURITY PROTOCOLS

- All away teams are to include at minimum one security officer whose chief responsibility is the safety of the team; though discouraged, the team's senior officer or the posting's commanding officer may countermand this protocol should circumstances warrant.

- Security officers are required to be armed on all away missions, customarily with the Type-II phaser. Orders from superior officers may countermand this protocol to restrict them to carrying a Type-I phaser or, though highly discouraged, no armament at all. Heavier weapons such as the Type-III phaser rifle are restricted to away missions in which hostile action is assured and only with the consent of the away team's senior officer.

- Security officers may take defensive action without the direction of the team's leader or any ranking officers should they feel a threat to the team's safety is imminent but may be ordered to stand down by a ranking officer should the ranking officer feel the situation can be peaceably resolved.

- Security officers are required to enforce Federation law during away missions on Federation worlds, spacecraft, or outposts and are mandated reporters and responders in the presence of illegal activity while on an away mission.

- Security officers on away missions to non-Federation worlds, allied or otherwise, are bound by the Prime Directive to adhere to the planet's laws and may only operate in furtherance of a security matter internal to the planet's culture with the consent of the planet's governmental representatives.

CRIMINAL INVESTIGATION

Starfleet security officers act as law enforcement officials within Federation space and at times find themselves investigating acts of an illicit nature, such as theft, smuggling, terrorism, and even murder, wherein the culprit is not immediately known and must be discovered and apprehended. A starship security officer is more likely to find themselves in such a mystery while visiting a planet, outpost, or starship where such acts have taken place, but, though Starfleet prides itself on its psychological screening processes, Starfleet's history is unfortunately marred with examples of officers who descended into criminal behavior either due to their base desires overriding their oath to Starfleet ideals or due to mental illness that robs them of their ability to distinguish right from wrong. Starbases are an even more likely posting where security officers may encounter a crime in need of investigation, since many starbases have a significant civilian population from all cultures, Federation and otherwise, and due to the transient traffic of ships that travel to and from the base.

COLLECTION AND ANALYSIS OF EVIDENCE

Every criminal investigation begins with an on-site view of the crime scene, wherein a security officer may see for themselves the end effects of the crime, such as the remains of a murder victim, the absence of valuables, and damage inflicted. The security officer, often in tandem with science division personnel, conducts a thorough analysis of the scene via tricorder scans (a **Reason +** Science Task) and visual inspection (a **Reason + Security Task**) for any details that may lead to uncovering those responsible. Gamemasters may raise difficulty on these to 2 or even 3 if the character opts to look through the crime scene for anything not obvious to the untrained eye, such as trace amounts of an out-of-place substance or subtle bodily alterations to a murder victim that would identify the cause of death. Players that earn instant Momentum may be rewarded with information they would have otherwise needed to succeed at another task roll to determine, while Complications rolled may result in something that would slow the investigation, such as the contamination of evidence or the loss of sensor logs containing footage of the crime scene.

FORENSIC AUTOPSY

Cursory post-mortem examinations of the deceased can easily be handled by tricorder scans conducted by a medical officer (a **Reason + Medical Task**), but if a death is suspicious or the cause not immediately obvious, a security officer may request that a forensic autopsy be performed. Gamemasters should treat such a process as an **Extended Reason + Medical Task**, with each Breakthrough yielding increasingly vital clues. Though autopsies are handled primarily by medical officers, the investigating security officer must still review the autopsy findings and interpret them

affected by the malady may be in a panic due to the length of time needed to develop a treatment or due to the isolation of quarantine, while those that have so far escaped affliction may have let their fear of becoming victims of the malady overtake their better natures, posing a peacekeeping challenge for security officers. With the aid of medical department colleagues, a security officer could potentially learn that the malady was deliberately introduced into the population for nefarious purposes.

NEAR SPACE EXPLORATION

This component category centers on plots set in the well-traveled Alpha and Beta Quadrants and worlds therein that are hubs of both culture and government, such as Earth, Qo'noS, and Romulus, as well as strategic outposts such as Deep Space 9. Security officers may be called to one of these locations to apply their expertise to a tactical dilemma such as an attack by hostile forces or a criminal investigation. Should the location be the security officer's homeworld or home colony, they may find themselves drawn there for more personal reasons. Perhaps a friend or family member has been accused of a crime and the security officer must determine their guilt or innocence, or their loved one may have fallen victim to violence, necessitating the officer's intervention.

PLANETARY EXPLORATION

Missions focused on the survey of an uncharted world have a role for security officers as well, as the unknown variables of exploring a newly discovered planet may pose any number of potential threats to an away team in the form of hostile sentient aliens, predatory indigenous animal life, or harmful natural phenomena such as severe weather or seismic activity. The safety of the away team is customarily the primary duty of the team's security officer, but the discovery of a threat to a peaceful indigenous culture may present a challenge to a security officer who wishes to formulate a defense.

RESEARCH

This category of plot component broadly deals with any form of personal research project, either spearheaded by a security officer or another officer either within or outside the security department that the security officer is assisting. A security officer may offer their expertise in terms of providing tactical expertise pertaining to a location crucial to the project or pointing out elements of the project that could compromise their safety or even the entire crew's.

against other evidence (**Reason + Security**). Gamemasters may allow a security character to successfully make correlative leaps of logic between autopsy reports and additional evidence on hand depending on the results of their rolls or if they opt to use Momentum or Determination.

SUSPECT AND WITNESS INTERVIEWS

A key element of any investigation of a crime is the collection of statements from witnesses and the questioning of potential suspects. Security officers skilled in the interview process are skilled in the arts of conversation and persuasion, as a major part of successfully interviewing witnesses and suspects is building a rapport with the interview subject to make them feel at ease and therefore sufficiently relaxed to speak freely or remember details of the crime the officer had not yet determined. Some skilled interviewers even have a practiced eye to watch for micro expressive tells that indicate that someone is hiding something. The base Task for conducting an interview in a criminal investigation is an **Opposed Insight + Security Task.**

ARREST

Once a security officer has compiled enough incriminating evidence against a suspect, they customarily submit the evidence to either their superior officer if they are investigating a crime in Federation territory or to the native law enforcement authority of the non-aligned planet they are assisting for approval of an arrest warrant. If the case takes place in Federation territory, the suspect is imprisoned in the ship's brig to await remand for trial; if the investigation was a joint effort with a non-aligned world, the perpetrator is remanded into the legal system of the planet's government, even if the perpetrator is a Federation citizen or a Starfleet officer.

USE OF PSIONIC ABILITIES

Information obtained from a subject through the use of psionic abilities such as Vulcan mind-meld or Betazoid telepathy or empathy is considered inadmissible as evidence according to Federation law, as telepathic or empathic impressions cannot be reliably recorded as a tangible piece of evidence, at least not with current technology, and whether or not the individual who obtained this information is telling the truth or filtering the information through their personal experiences and biases cannot be concretely verified. Empaths and telepaths working within Starfleet may determine that a suspect in a crime is hiding something based on surface thoughts and may suggest to investigating officers that the suspect is worth further scrutiny, but Federation law forbids Starfleet officers with these abilities to probe their minds without consent, both due to the inadmissibility of any information obtained and violation of Starfleet ethics. Gamemasters should caution Players of the above should they seek to take a shortcut of this nature and the disciplinary consequences should they proceed.

GOLD PLOT COMPONENTS

Gold plot components are focused on combat and physical action, narrative elements tailor-made for security officers. With the training security officers receive in both personal and ship-scale combat, Gamemasters should have little difficulty applying a gold plot component to a narrative intended to focus of security department characters.

Use this random table to generate a quick gold plot component to incorporate into your adventure or generate a story idea for your security Player Characters.

GENERATING GOLD PLOT COMPONENTS

D20 ROLL	GOLD PLOT COMPONENT
1–5	Defense
6–9	Escort
10–12	Espionage
13–16	Patrol
17–20	Tactical

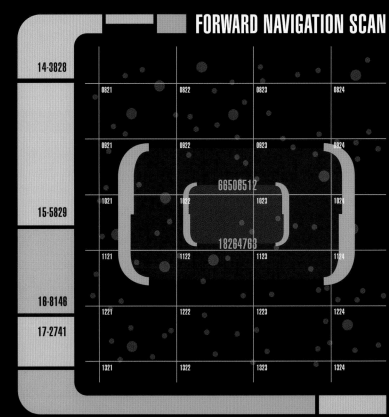

FORWARD NAVIGATION SCAN

DEFENSE

Defense plots fall squarely within the operational purview of the security department, whether dealing with defending something tangible such as a single person, a security officer's crew, or the Federation at large, or an abstract idea such as a principle or idea important to the Player Character. Security officers' primary duty is to defend Federation citizens, whether at the controls of a starship's tactical systems or facing a hostile enemy in personal combat.

ESCORT

During escort missions, a security officer becomes an important part of the undertaking, as Starfleet vessels are often tasked to shepherd civilian transports with minimal or no defensive capabilities, which would mean having to take the transport's position and welfare into consideration during a battle as well as their own ship. A security officer may also be called upon to board a ship being escorted, either to inspect the ship's cargo to search for contraband or to determine why hostile craft have taken an interest in the transport. Reasons could include something as simple as precious cargo or perhaps a ship's being targeted due to a vendetta against the ship's crew or a single member thereof.

ESPIONAGE

Security officers, particularly those with intelligence backgrounds, are ideal for covert operations missions as their skills at tactically analyzing any given situation, even in politically hostile territory, increases the chance of everyone participating the mission making it home alive. Covert operations are by no means an easy or safe mission profile, however; security officers may be placed undercover in unsafe areas of a non-aligned planet or assigned to infiltrate a criminal gang or terrorist organization and may be compelled to perform far outside the confines of Starfleet ethics or even Federation law, to the detriment of their ideals and sometimes their mental health. Some covert operations missions are less taxing on the moral compass, though; security officers may be inserted into a Federation dignitary's entourage to act as a bodyguard or form a rescue team dispatched to recover hostages from unfriendly territory.

PATROL

Patrol missions have security officers on constant alert, particularly tactical officers assigned to bridge duty, as they are tasked with maintaining constant watch on the ship's sector for anything that may merit investigation. Security officers are tasked with not only surveying their assigned sector for potential threats or suspicious activity, but maintaining the ship's combat readiness should an out-of-the-ordinary sensor reading become something worthy of ordering the ship to red alert.

TACTICAL

Though Starfleet prefers that encounters with hostile starships or installations be defused with diplomacy, an adversary may often take that option out of consideration by initiating hostilities. A skilled tactical officer can make the difference between a satisfactory end of hostilities and a mass exodus to the escape pods, and a skilled bridge crew provide numerous advantages to the tactical officer during armed engagements.

The Gamemaster should also take into consideration the tactical strength of their adversary; if the ship is little more than a modified freighter with outdated or low-powered weaponry, play up the lessened sense of dread as well as the incredulousness and even potential comedy of such a

PERSONAL LOG

LIEUTENANT (JUNIOR GRADE) WORF, USS ENTERPRISE NCC-1701-D, STARDATE 41602.2

Lieutenant Yar… Tasha… died today.

From the away team's reports, she died as she had lived, performing her duties in defiance of the creature that ended her life as she attempted to reach Counselor Troi and Lieutenant Prieto's shuttlecraft. She faced her death with courage.

And yet, I find myself disquieted. My place was on the bridge, as was my duty. Still… I should have been there. I have read the reports. This thing… Armus… was impervious to phaser fire. It could kill with a gesture. It could have killed all of them if it so chose. Still, for Tasha to have been struck down and not being there facing her murderer feels wrong. It would have been an honorable death. A death befitting her sacrifice.

Captain Picard has installed me as her replacement. The security team is holding a wake for her in Ten-Forward. I will attend, to meet them, to share stories of Tasha, and to tell them that I shall lead them with honor, as she would have wished. Though I regret not facing her murderer on the field of battle, I will honor her passing by continuing her work in defense of Starfleet, of the Federation, and of the *Enterprise*.

Qapla', Natasha. While you were not a Klingon, you were a true warrior. Perhaps we shall meet again in the halls of *Sto-Vo-Kor*.

The Starfleet Academy curriculum provides training in a unified form of close-quarters unarmed combat combining elements from martial arts styles from across the Federation, with security track cadets receiving more advanced training in this form of unarmed combat. Starfleet personnel may choose to supplement their combat training by studying one or more additional martial arts styles, either to improve their combat skills, to compete in competitive martial arts events, or simply as a form of physical exercise.

Combat-oriented martial arts typically fall into one of three broad categories of fighting technique or a combination of multiple categories:

- **Striking styles** that emphasize direct physical attacks with a part of the body. Examples include the fist-fighting art of boxing, and the East Asian martial arts of kickboxing, taekwondo, karate, and muay thai, all of which train practitioners in a variety of hand, foot, knee, and elbow strikes.

- **Grappling styles** that focus on the subdual or immobilization of an opponent using a variety of body throws and jointlocks that employ a combination of leverage and manipulation of bodily pressure points. Examples include Greco-Roman wrestling, the East Asian arts of judo and sumo, Brazilian jiu-jitsu, the Russian grappling technique sambo, and aikido, the Japanese art of grappling that emphasizes the redirection of an opponent's attacks and peaceful subjugation of an opponent without causing injury. Aikido is a favorite among Starfleet security personnel due to its ability to force compliance from an adversary without causing undue physical harm.

- **Weapon-based styles** that train the practitioner in the use of a specific melee weapon, usually a blade or polearm. Examples include the Japanese swordplay form of kendo, competitive fencing, archery, and the use of any sort of sword, quarterstaff, knife, or flail, wielded singly or in pairs depending on the weapon. The use of Klingon bladed weapons such as the *bat'leth*, *mek'leth*, and *d'k tahg* and the Andorian dueling code of *Ushaan*, all of which are described in the core rulebook, would also fall into this category.

Following is a sampling of martial arts styles native to *Star Trek* fiction to complement the examples listed above.

- **Anbo-jyutsu:** Touted by its practitioners as the "ultimate evolution of the martial arts," anbo-jyutsu is a competitive weapon-based martial art of Human origin wherein two adversaries clad in protective armor and helmets with opaque face masks that render them sightless face one another in a raised circular ring using modified polearms. Each staff is fitted with a proximity sensor at one end that emits a sound when near the opponent's staff sensor, enabling the combatants to locate one another using their hearing and deliver strikes or sweeping attacks. Anbo-jyutsu practitioners gain not only prowess in the use of polearms but an increased sense of situational awareness through practiced use of their other four senses while blinded.

- **Mok'bara:** A Klingon grappling and striking style that emphasizes the redirection of an opponent's attack to move them into the path of a bare-handed strike. To Human martial arts scholars, *mok'bara* appears to combine techniques used both in aikido and T'ai chi ch'üan, a Chinese martial arts form that evolved into a means of meditation. *Mok'bara* is the basis for all Klingon martial arts and can be practiced alone or in organized classes.

- **Suus Mahna:** A Vulcan form of unarmed combat that focused on defensive and evasive techniques that were still effective in incapacitating adversaries. *Suus mahna*, which takes years to master, also uses the inherent logic of the Vulcan mind to read an opponent's body language to anticipate their next move.

NEW TASKS

The following Tasks supplement those in *Chapter 7* of the core rulebook and reflect the techniques of the martial arts forms listed above.

- **Redirect:** The character redirects an incoming unarmed attack so that the attacker finds themselves at a disadvantage. If the character succeeds, their attacker forfeits any actions on the next turn, reducing the Difficulty on the defending character's next attack against the opponent to 0.

- **Non-Lethal Attack:** The character attempts to use the blunt portion of a bladed weapon to incapacitate rather than kill. If the character succeeds, the weapon's Vicious Quality is ignored. If the character rolls a Complication, the Vicious Quality remains in effect.

- **Immobilize:** Through the use of a jointlock or other martial arts technique, the character attempts to force an opponent into a state of submission using a **Fitness + Security Task** against an identical Task rolled by the opponent. If successful, the character has their opponent pinned down and unable to take any actions apart from trying to escape the hold each turn with an Opposed **Fitness + Security Tasks.** However, with the character occupied with immobilizing their opponent, they forfeit any defensive Task in response to attacks from other attackers, reducing attack Tasks against them to Difficulty 0. If another attacker succeeds, the character is forced to release the hold.

ship taking on a crew of Starfleet's finest. Conversely, in the face of something akin to a *D'deridex*-class warbird or a Borg cube, the Gamemaster should stress the ominousness of the situation and make the crew feel that they are one wrong move from their characters' families receiving condolence letters.

Tactical officers depend on far more than the phasers, torpedo launchers, and deflector shields to help them combat a hostile threat. Each of the bridge officers with which the tactical officer works can provide valuable assistance, enabling their Players to lead Tasks or assist the tactical officer to enhance their chances of succeeding and ending the battle with their ship in one piece.

- **Commanding Officer:** The posting's captain can assist a tactical officer by calling on the career experiences that led him to his current position (**Reason + Security**).

- **Communications:** The communications officer can monitor signal traffic from an adversary's ship to advise the tactical officer of impending actions or calls for reinforcements (**Control + Engineering**).

- **Helm and Navigator:** The flight control officer may coordinate the ship's maneuvers with the tactical officer to evade incoming fire, to keep an adversary from attacking weakened shields, or to provide a better firing arc for the starship's weapons (**Control + Conn**).

- **Internal Systems Control:** The bridge officer that oversees internal systems can advise the tactical officer of any effects to the ship's operation suffered from battle damage (**Reason + Engineering**).

- **Security Oversight:** Though the tactical officer customarily handles this role on the bridge (as of the *Enterprise* and Next Generation Eras), security NPCs may notify the tactical officer of hostile intruders that boarded the ship while in combat (**Reason + Security**).

- **Sensor Operations:** The science officer may use the ship's sensors to detect any weaknesses in a hostile ship the tactical officer may exploit (**Reason + Science**).

USING THE OPERATIONS DIVISION
ENGINEERING DEPARTMENT STORYLINES

"TO HENRY ARCHER. I WONDER WHAT HE WOULD HAVE THOUGHT IF HE KNEW HIS ENGINE WAS GONNA HELP SAVE THE HUMAN RACE."

— COMMANDER CHARLES TUCKER III

RED PLOT COMPONENTS

Red plot components thrust engineers into scenarios that center on the delicacies of interaction with friendly and unfriendly powers, be they Federation bureaucrats, the government of an unaligned planet, or the captain of a hostile vessel. Though typically the realm of command department officers, the cross-training afforded to Starfleet officers would amply see them through these scenarios, Starfleet engineers can easily apply their technological acumen towards such situations, and the outcome of a red plot component could potentially hinge on an engineer's expertise.

Use this random table to generate a quick red plot component to incorporate into your adventure or generate a story idea for your engineering Player Characters.

GENERATING RED PLOT COMPONENTS

D20 ROLL	RED PLOT COMPONENT
1	Conspiracy
2–6	Diplomacy
7–11	First Contact
12–14	Political
15–17	Show the Flag
18–19	Spiritual
20	Starfleet JAG

CONSPIRACIES

An engineer may be called upon to help investigate a suspected conspiracy within Starfleet or the Federation, perhaps to investigate damage to a starship or starbase that resulted from wrongdoing within the posting's crew or committed by high-ranking officers. For example, an engineer could be assigned

BEYOND THE FINAL FRONTIER

Following is a further expansion of the plot component element illustrated in *Chapter 5.10 Security Department Storylines*, this time providing plot components geared towards engineering department Player Characters.

to investigate the catastrophic failure of an experimental device and learn that the failure was due to a fault that was disregarded or covered up by the device's developers, the Starfleet officers overseeing its development, or even both for the sake of preventing the fault from derailing its development.

DIPLOMACY

Engineers could conceivably become involved in matters of diplomacy, as the assessment of a culture's technology could play into and potentially sway the outcome of sensitive negotiations. For instance, an engineer may be tasked to investigate a form of technology native to one culture that another culture either covets and wishes to negotiate for its use or, conversely, considers it a potential or existing threat that the engineer must either confirm or disprove. An engineer might even belong to one of two cultures involved in pitched negotiations with whom their crew has become involved.

FIRST CONTACT

The assessment of a newly encountered culture's technological development is often an operational priority in the case of first contact situations, as a culture's level of technology is one of the criteria by which the Federation determines if a culture merits contact, particularly if the culture has no knowledge of sentient life beyond that of their own world. An engineer might also be

EPISODES FOCUSED ON ENGINEERING CHALLENGES

"MINEFIELD" (ENTERPRISE)

Enterprise-NX is disabled by a cloaked Romulan mine and must affect repairs while attempting to remove another mine from the ship's hull without detonating it.

"THE ULTIMATE COMPUTER" (THE ORIGINAL SERIES)

The *Enterprise* is fitted with an experimental computer system designed to fully automate starship functions, but the crew must find a way to disable the computer when it begins taking paranoid, life-threatening actions.

"BOOBY TRAP" (THE NEXT GENERATION)

The *Enterprise*-D falls victim to a derelict Promellian ship that disables the ship's drive systems and threatens to flood the ship with lethal radiation. Geordi La Forge consults with a hologram of one the *Enterprise*'s designers to determine how to restore the warp drive and allow them to escape.

"CIVIL DEFENSE" (DEEP SPACE NINE)

Deep Space 9's crew and population lose control of the station and are trapped aboard when a Cardassian security protocol designed to quell a Bajoran uprising is accidentally triggered.

"DREADNOUGHT" (VOYAGER)

An artificially intelligent missile deployed by B'Elanna Torres during her Maquis days is found in the Delta Quadrant within striking distance of an inhabited planet, forcing Torres to beam aboard the large missile in an attempt to disarm it.

---

tasked to investigate unfamiliar forms of technology employed by a newly encountered culture to evaluate such technologies for their value to the Federation, potential risks to sentient life, and their adherence to Federation law.

POLITICAL

Technology is often a focus of a political dilemma; for instance, the laws of most Alpha and Beta Quadrant cultures prohibit the manufacture and distribution of biogenic weaponry, and one of the stipulations of the Treaty of Algeron, signed following the Tomed Incident in 2311, prohibited the Federation government from developing cloaking technology. Engineers could be drawn into a story of political intrigue wherein they are tasked to assist on a project that, either known or unknown to them, leads to the development of a banned technology. An engineer may also be called to evaluate whether a banned technology was used to engineer a catastrophic event that threatens to ignite tensions or even potentially war between two rival powers, one of which could be the Federation.

SHOW THE FLAG

Starfleet is sometimes assigned to fairly but firmly establish its authority within its borders, either to citizens of member worlds or colonies or to those of unaligned or hostile governments. As with political plot elements, an engineer may have cause to determine whether a banned technology is being developed in violation of Federation law. Engineers might also be tasked to aid in the repair of vital facilities or services damaged or destroyed due to a conflict within a member world's population or from outside attack.

SPIRITUAL

Though their work is often the antithesis of spiritualism, engineering officers may have their own superstitions or beliefs when it comes to their ship or starbase, which could be played upon by Gamemasters depending on their relevance. Engineering characters may also try to rationalize spiritual experiences, investigating them alongside science officers.

STARFLEET JAG

An engineer may be recruited by the Judge Advocate General's office to analyze a critical technological failure to determine whether the failure was the result of equipment failure or the result of negligence at the hands of an officer under JAG investigation. The JAG could also potentially target an engineering Player Character as a suspect in such an investigation as well, forcing them to self-evaluate their actions prior to the disaster to determine whether they were legitimately at fault, the event was the unavoidable result of faulty equipment or materials, or if the failure was engineered as a result of sabotage by another party.

BLUE PLOT COMPONENTS

Blue plot components focus primarily on science and technology and, therefore, provide ample narrative foundations to Starfleet engineers. Engineering officers have a strong level of cross-training in the theoretical sciences as a foundation for their tutelage in their core disciplines.

Use this random table to generate a quick blue plot component to incorporate into your adventure or generate a story idea for your engineering Player Characters.

GENERATING BLUE PLOT COMPONENTS

D20 ROLL	BLUE PLOT COMPONENT
1–5	Deep Space Exploration
6–7	Evacuation
8–9	Medical Issue
10–14	Near Space Exploration
15–17	Planetary Exploration
18–20	Research

DEEP SPACE EXPLORATION

One of the primary mandates of Starfleet is to explore uncharted space to discover new worlds and cultures. Engineers are a vital part of that mandate as their expertise is often needed to shore up a ship's systems against the effects of spatial phenomena or to analyze technology abandoned in space. An engineer and a ship's science officer may often be called to work in tandem to analyze a newly discovered cosmic phenomenon and determine whether it presents a danger to the ship and her crew.

Key to the operation of any Starfleet ship or base is its capacity to receive, process, store, and transmit information, whether this is transmitted internally through a computer core, optical data network, and internal sensors, or collected by the sophisticated sensor arrays that act as the starship or starbase's eyes and ears of their surroundings in the void of space. Engineers expert in this technology ensure that a ship's crew is well informed by internal and external data sources. This enables science officers to make use of the sensors for research purposes, flight control officers to plot courses, and tactical officers to assess surroundings for potential threats.

EVACUATION

In the event of missions where a ship, outpost, or planet must be evacuated due to political pressure or a cataclysm either impending or in progress, the engineer's role may be to help prepare their ship to take on evacuees or, in conjunction with the sciences department, to analyze the event dooming the population to either develop a means of counteracting the event or at least establish a timeline by which the ship can begin evacuation procedures.

Though transporter technology became the safest means of travel by *The Next Generation* era, transporter accidents of all sorts have occurred throughout recorded history. Accidents have played a key role in many *Star Trek* episodes, and Gamemasters are encouraged to occasionally build a story about this seemingly innocuous travel tool becoming more than a source of inconvenience for their characters.

MEDICAL ISSUE

A widespread medical issue that has afflicted the population of a world, ship, or outpost poses a challenge for more than a crew's medical staff. Engineers may be tasked to build containment facilities to quarantine the infected, either on the ship or at the site of the epidemic. An engineer may also be needed to restore services such as power distribution and communications that fell into disrepair due to the epidemic.

NEAR SPACE EXPLORATION

This component category centers on plots set in the well-traveled Alpha and Beta Quadrants and worlds therein that are hubs of both culture and government, such as Earth, Qo'noS, and Romulus, as well as strategic outposts such as Deep Space 9. An engineer may find themselves drawn to one of these worlds or even their homeworld, either in a

WORKING WITH THE SCIENCE DEPARTMENT

Starfleet engineers are, in effect, scientists in their own right, the key difference from their sciences division colleagues being that engineers apply their scientific know-how towards its practical application through the development, construction, modification, and repair of technology and physical materials. Starfleet engineers often work closely with science and medical officers in order to ensure that their work meets sound scientific standards and that the work will not only perform its intended function but that it will either be free of malfunction or at least resistant to it. Below is a breakdown of how each broad category of the sciences may assist with engineering challenges using Assist Tasks and applicable Focuses.

- An engineer will often consult with **physical scientists** in terms of a piece of technology's material composition in order to ensure that the device will be able to handle external stresses and be able to perform its assigned task without succumbing to the forces with which it works. **Example Focuses:** *Astronomy, Astrophysics, Chemistry, Physics, Spatial Phenomena.*

- The expertise of **planetary scientists** may be sought for civil engineering projects to help evaluate a project's effect on a planet's environment and whether it can withstand environmental stresses. **Example Focuses:** *Climatology, Geology, Oceanography.*

- **Life scientists** may be consulted to determine if a piece of technology is potentially harmful to sentients. Engineers may also work with medical officers during development and implantation of artificial limbs or organs. **Example Focuses:** *Biochemistry, Botany, Neuroscience, Toxicology, Xenobiology.*

- **Formal scientists** are often sought for their expertise in developing and debugging the operational software of a new invention, or decoding or unencrypting the software of an existing device. **Example Focuses:** *Computer Science, Logic, Mathematics.*

A Starfleet vessel may be called to survey a derelict spacecraft, to either determine the reason the ship came to be in that condition, or if the cause is already known, to inspect the damage and evaluate if the ship can be restored to operation. Gamemasters are encouraged to play up the inherent danger of boarding a derelict starship; while the trip could be an uneventful educational survey, the dark confines of a dead spacecraft could hide an unseen threat potentially lethal to a recovery team and their ship's crew.

- **Environmental Systems Failure:** Depending on the event that led to the ship floating adrift in the stars, the possibility that the ship is not only uninhabited but uninhabitable is very likely. The collapse of a vessel's environmental systems could mean that the ship has no breathable air or heat, the artificial gravity plating may be offline, or more often than not both. This will require a salvage team to wear EV suits and make use of the suits' magnetic boots to traverse the ship safely.

- **Propulsion and Power Systems Failure:** Conventional wisdom would lead many to assume that a derelict spacecraft would have inoperable drive and power transfer systems, and that in and of itself would pose minimal risk to a recovery team, but the cause of the failure and potential side effects are something a recovery team would have to face and overcome. Any number of chemical and radiological hazards, such as damaged reactor shielding or a warp core coolant leak, resulting from a failure of the power distribution or propulsion systems could pose a threat to a recovery team.

- **Computer Systems Failure:** A derelict's computer system being offline could potentially pose no further threat to a recovery team than a minor inconvenience due to being unable to use the ship's computer to run systems diagnostics or search for clues as to what happened to the ship and her crew. Then again, perhaps the computer system was the cause for the calamity due to malware installed by a hostile unknown party or a security protocol that malfunctioned and considered the crew hostile intruders. A recovery team would do well to be very careful in attempting to get a derelict's computer online, though the potential ramifications of doing so may make for an excellent plot point upon which the Gamemaster can build a story.

- **Hull Breaches:** Though an EV suit will protect a recovery team engineer from the lack of an internal Class M environment, hull breaches pose other dilemmas for recovery teams. Interstellar debris and cosmic phenomena are capable of getting inside the ship and potentially harming a team member. Part of the ship could be completely obliterated to the point that traveling from one point to the other requires a zero-g push-off through empty space if no alternate route can be found. Also, hull fragments could float weightlessly throughout the ship, proving a hazard to the team if the hull fragments are sharp enough to slice through an EV suit.

- **Xenobiological Infestation:** If the crew were killed by whatever disabled the ship, their remains may pose a biohazard if the crew's species emit microorganisms harmful to other sentients during the decomposition process or whatever else happens to the species' remains post-mortem. Perhaps the ship fell victim to a viral contagion that still permeates the ship's interior even without the benefit of atmosphere. Or perhaps something else is on board the ship, one or more specimens of another sapient species, the things that killed the crew that have waited an eternity for new victims…

Presuming the recovery team returns to their ship without incident or at least alive, the supervising engineer may make recommendations regarding what to do with the derelict. If it is deemed safe or if any dangers can be stemmed, the engineer may recommend that the derelict be tractored to a starbase or shipyard for further study. However, if the derelict's risk to sentient life outweighs the desire for scientific discovery, the engineer may recommend that the derelict be destroyed.

professional capacity, wherein they may attend a symposium that has caught their interest or their expertise is needed by either a family member or old friend, or as a more personal journey, such as the death of a beloved relative or a reunion with an old love or a bitter rival that narratively plays into the game's main plot.

PLANETARY EXPLORATION

Away missions to unexplored planets are tailor-made for engineers, as one is often needed to make sure the away team's equipment is always in working order and to evaluate the technology of any indigenous culture the away team may encounter on the surface. Engineers should also be on hand for the discovery and analysis of alien artifacts found on an unexplored world; see p.81 and the accompanying sidebar for Starfleet regulations on the handling of technology of unknown origin.

RESEARCH

This category covers any science- or technology-related wherein the Player Character becomes greatly invested in the research of a particular subject of interest, either on their own or aiding a fellow officer or personal acquaintance. An engineer could assist a science officer

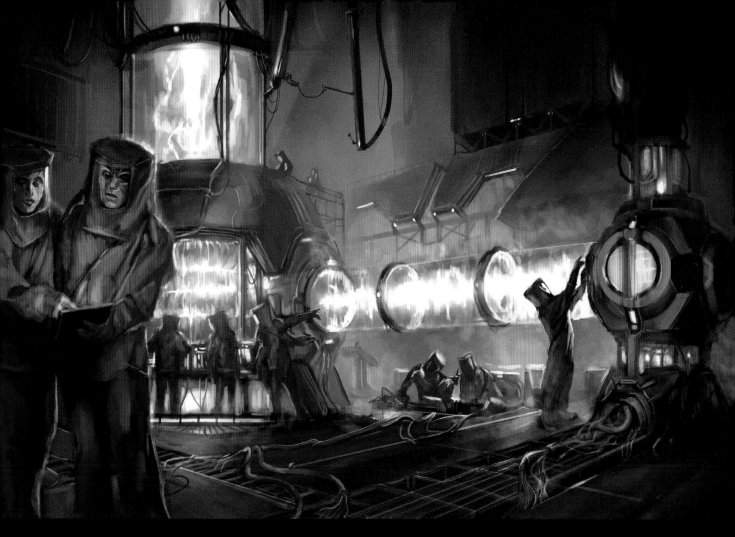

in analyzing a form of technology or scientific phenomena either newly discovered or long-known yet cloaked in mystery. The engineer could even develop and construct new equipment to assist in the research.

GOLD PLOT COMPONENTS

Gold plot components center on physical action and combat either personal or ship-based. Engineers are often found deep in the guts of a ship's systems during a battle, making sure that power is rerouted where it needs to go, that damaged sections of the ship are sealed off, and that the ship's defensive systems remain in working order. Starfleet engineers are well known for maintaining focus on their jobs even in the heat of a firefight and are as much a key to surviving a battle as the tactical officer on the bridge.

Use this random table to generate a quick gold plot component to incorporate into your adventure or generate a story idea for your engineering Player Characters.

GENERATING GOLD PLOT COMPONENTS

D20 ROLL	GOLD PLOT COMPONENT
1–5	Defense
6–9	Escort
10–12	Espionage
13–16	Patrol
17–20	Tactical

DEFENSE

This category is a catch-all for any plot focusing on the broad concept of defense, be it defending others in danger or a Player Character defending themselves, their ship, or their crew. As stated above, Starfleet engineers are trained to develop solutions to engineering challenges under stress and play a vital part in making sure that their crew successfully defends themselves or others from opposing forces. Gamemasters should tailor defense plot elements to not only an engineer's ability to keep existing equipment operational during a crisis but to their talent for innovating out-of-the-box solutions on the fly.

ESCORT

As the escort of unarmed transport vessels is often a duty for which a Starfleet vessel can be assigned, an engineer can be very useful if a ship being escorted suffers a mechanical failure necessitating their expertise. Gamemasters are encouraged to play up the comparative technology levels of an escorted ship. Many civilian transports are manufactured by shipyards lacking the resources, the technology, or the care of craftsmanship Starfleet's yards have at hand, so an engineer may find themselves on something that makes even the most spartan of Starfleet vessels look like a luxury liner in comparison. A Gamemaster may modify Difficulty or Complication range of any Task needed to repair malfunctions or damage to a ship that may not have as robust equipment as the average Starfleet ship.

ESPIONAGE

The employment of covert operations to ascertain the movements of unaligned or hostile governments is a duty most in the Federation would consider distasteful, but missions of espionage prove themselves necessary and useful time and again. An engineer could easily act as a covert operative by portraying themselves as a simple mechanic aboard a freighter or on an unaligned colony. Engineers could also be employed as operational support for field agents by providing technical support for their equipment.

PATROL

Patrol duty involves assigning a vessel to survey a designated sector of space for anything out of the ordinary, be it previously uncharted spatial phenomena, the movements of unaligned or unidentified vessels within the sector, or the presence of anything that raises suspicion. An engineer may be called upon to analyze sensor scans of a vessel passing through the sector for anything amiss, or be added to an away team dispatched to board a vessel that the ship's captain has ordered searched.

TACTICAL

Keeping a starship or starbase running at optimal levels during normal operations is a tall order, but place that same posting in a firefight with a belligerent adversary intent on blasting it out of the stars, and an engineer's job becomes that much more complicated and even more crucial. Depending on how badly the battle fares, a chief engineer must direct damage control teams throughout the posting to repair crippled systems and seal hull breaches, all while maintaining a constant watch for newly inflicted damage in need of repair.

Situations such as this can become a delicate balancing act, as a chief engineer may be stretched thin on resources and manpower and find themselves deciding which of the damaged key systems need repair first. Do they redirect the damage control teams to shore up the shields, or would they be better utilized restoring life support to the three decks who just lost it? And what if the attacking vessel strikes the ship in such a way that prevents a damage control team from reaching the affected system, or worse, incapacitates or kills them?

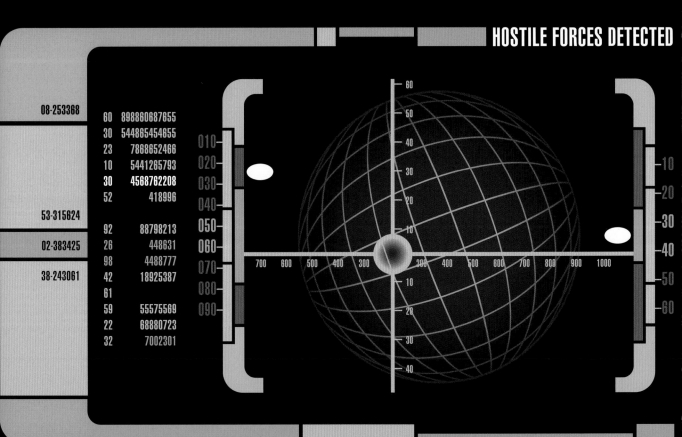

DIAGNOSTICS

Starfleet engineers routinely run diagnostic tests of the various systems they maintain. These diagnostics have level designations that identify the labor involved and estimated time of completion:

- **Level 1:** The most laborious of the diagnostic levels. The system being examined is entirely shut down and subjected to extensive automated analysis with all work performed on site where the equipment is in use. Estimated completion time: several hours.

- **Level 2:** Less extensive variation of the Level 1 diagnostic that requires less on-site monitoring and takes approximately half the time (a few hours).

- **Level 3:** A lesser diagnostic that requires on-site monitoring of only the more important elements of a system. Estimated completion time: ten minutes.

- **Level 4:** An automated verification that a system is suffering no malfunctions. Estimated completion time: less than thirty seconds.

- **Level 5:** A minor and routine automated systems check meant simply to verify performance; this is typically performed once a day for each system. Estimated completion time: less than 2 seconds.

ALIEN TECHNOLOGIES

As stated in *Chapter 2: Operations Division*, the Starfleet Corps of Engineers are often called in to evaluate technological devices of unknown origin that are discovered by various means, usually through research digs conducted by archaeologists or anthropologists that have uncovered something no one has seen for centuries or even millennia, if ever. While such a discovery would interest the SCE, a ship manned by Player Characters may be in closer proximity to the discovery site and may opt to answer the call out of scientific curiosity. The basic rules for technological experimentation and the grades of technology in terms of its relative level of advancement are discussed at length in *Chapter 8: Technology and Equipment* in the core rulebook.

If responding to a call to examine a newly found item of alien technology, an engineer must adhere to all Starfleet safety protocols for dealing with technology of unknown origin, which are listed in the sidebar in *Chapter 2* on p.26. Starfleet treats every newly discovered technological item effectively as an unexploded bomb, regardless of its seeming innocuousness or lack of internal activity, and Starfleet engineers must keep their scientific curiosity in check to ensure that activation of or tampering with the device constitutes no risk to the lives of the crew or any sentient life in the vicinity of the object.

Once the object has been deemed safe to physically approach and the crew's ship and equipment are modified to repel electronic tampering should the item have such a capability, an engineer may beam down with an away team, either as the senior officer or subordinate to a superior, and conduct numerous tests to determine the object's origin, age, purpose, and potential value to science using Tasks combining either Control, Reason, or Daring with Engineering or Science, with Difficulties and Complication Ranges set by the Gamemaster as defined in the rules for technology of unfamiliar design listed in *Chapter 8* of the core rulebook.

Example: *An away team from the* U.S.S. Shenlong, *led by chief engineer Lieutenant Commander Stephanie Morse, has arrived to assess a sphere of unknown origin unearthed on Beta Selanis II. Morse learns from her tricorder with one success on a **Control + Science Task** that the unfamiliar symbols on the sphere emit a warmer temperature than the rest of the sphere, but that the sphere is emitting no overt signs of internal power. Morse attempts to touch the symbols which prompts her Gamemaster to have her roll a **Daring + Science Task** with Difficulty 2 and a Complication Range of 2. The GM has a nasty surprise within the sphere for Lieutenant Commander Morse should she roll a Complication…*

Should the object be deemed safe and of benefit to scientific study, the supervising engineer should notify their commanding officer and recommend that (based on whether the discovery site is on a Federation world and, if not, that permission is sought by the planet's government) to either set up a research post to further examine the object or, if possible, to remove the object from the discovery site and transport it to the nearest Federation institute of learning or research firm.

If at any time before or during the away team's survey the supervising engineer discovers that the object in whole or in part is a risk to sentient life that is beyond the away team's ability to stop once triggered, the primary focus of the survey is shifted away from scientific study and towards the safe disposal of the device. The supervising engineer must then determine a method of removing the object from the discovery site or destroying it without triggering any internal failsafes or risking the lives of the away team or any native population the planet may house.

The *Star Trek Adventures* core rulebook details the Damage Control Task by which a chief engineer, with a successful **Presence + Engineering Task**, can direct damage control teams to repair systems damaged in combat and eliminate damage penalties. The chief engineer may opt to take the Minor Action Change Position if they wish to affect repairs to the affected system himself rather than direct repair efforts from the bridge or main engineering. If doing so while in combat, the chief engineer may find himself at an increased level of difficulty for a variety of reasons.

STRUCTURAL DAMAGE

Damage to internal or external structure can pose a problem for repair efforts if the damage prevents repair teams from reaching a system in need of repair. Bulkhead debris could fill the adjoining corridor, the hull could be close to a breach not far from the damaged system's location, or the area of the ship or base is housing the damaged system has been exposed to space with only force fields keeping in the internal atmosphere. Engineers may have to find ways around or through these obstructions with additional Tasks before they can attempt the Task themselves.

Example: *Ensign Vorik is racing through the corridors of the U.S.S. Voyager to the severed EPS conduit feeding the forward deflector shield generators in order to repair it before the Hirogen warship Voyager is engaged with makes its next attack run. Just as Vorik rounds the corner to where the conduit is, he runs into a pile of debris from the deck above caving in that completely cuts him off from the conduit. Resigned to his fate, Vorik begins rolling towards an* **Extended Control + Engineering Task** *to cut his way through the wreckage with a plasma torch, hoping to have enough of it cleared so he can reach and repair the conduit before another Hirogen weapons burst slices into Voyager's hull…*

HAZARDOUS MATERIALS

The systems of a starship or starbase require the use of energies and chemicals that are inherently unsafe to biological life, hence the multiple safety systems Starfleet employs in their vessels and outposts. Battle damage, however, can cause a failure of these safety systems, putting the crew at sometimes deadly risk of exposure to deadly radiation or volatile substances, requiring damage control teams to spend precious seconds taking safety precautions before entering into pools or clouds of harmful materials.

Example: *As the battle rages between Voyager and the Hirogen warship, chief engineer Lieutenant B'Elanna Torres is with several of her subordinates in main engineering attempting to reroute power reserves to the ship's shields when a collapsing bulkhead shatters one of the warp core coolant tanks, pouring the lethally caustic fluid into main engineering. Torres orders everyone out of main engineering for their safety and withdraws from the room herself, preventing her from accessing engineering controls from that area of the ship. Torres has a few options: she could vent the coolant from the room using the environmental systems, order her staff into EV suits, or abandon main engineering for the time being and run repair efforts from the bridge using the Change Position Task, each of which cost her time neither she nor the Voyager crew may have to spare.*

WEAPON IMPACTS

Repairing the systems of a starship or starbase often requires surgical precision, and doing so in the heat of a firefight with a hostile craft only exacerbates an already difficult task. Every impact of a phaser beam or a photon torpedo causes a noticeable jolt that the posting's inertial dampers fail to compensate and that can cause anyone attempting a Task with fine motor skills a great deal of difficulty, which the Gamemaster can illustrate by affecting the Difficulty and potentially the Complication Range of the Task rolls involved.

Example: *Ensign Lyndsay Ballard is on Voyager's bridge attempting to reroute the ship's ODN lines to the targeting sensors, which the last volley of Hirogen weapons bursts disabled. Ballard has had to physically cut the ODN cable and splice in a bypass via an* **Extended Control + Engineering Task***, but before Ballard can make the last of her Task rolls, the Hirogen ship takes its turn in the combat and strikes Voyager's aft shields again, violently shaking the ship. The Gamemaster not only maintains Ballard's previous Difficulty of 2 for this Task but also increases her Complication Range by 1 due to being shaken by the impact, meaning that a roll of 19 or greater could cause further damage and impair Voyager's chances of surviving the battle, much less retaliating.*

CHAPTER 06.00

OPERATIONS PERSONNEL

9843698
2359873625927

06.10	STARFLEET INTELLIGENCE	084
06.20	STARFLEET CORPS OF ENGINEERS	087
06.30	STARFLEET PERSONNEL	090
06.40	SUPPORTING CHARACTERS	093

OPERATIONS PERSONNEL
STARFLEET INTELLIGENCE

"ALL I CAN DO IS READ THESE FASCINATING REPORTS AND ANALYSES, AND ANALYSES OF ANALYSES, AND THEN KEEP IT ALL TO MYSELF. BECAUSE NO ONE ELSE HAS A 'NEED TO KNOW.'"

— DOCTOR JULIAN BASHIR

OVERVIEW

During their voyages the crew of a starship will occasionally encounter members of Starfleet Intelligence. This section presents several such characters that Gamemasters can use in their campaigns.

ADMIRAL RANER [NOTABLE NPC]

Admiral Raner served as the head of Starfleet Security until 2370, when she was dishonorably discharged for restarting the covert program to develop a phasing cloaking device, a project Starfleet Intelligence had covered up several years before. As chief of Starfleet Security her remit covered the security and safety of the Federation, instigating criminal investigations, and guarding Starfleet and civilian facilities across Federation space.

TRAITS: Human, Flag Officer

VALUES:
- Safeguard the Federation from All Threats

ATTRIBUTES

CONTROL 08	FITNESS 08	PRESENCE 11
DARING 08	INSIGHT 09	REASON 10

DISCIPLINES

COMMAND 04	SECURITY 03	SCIENCE 01
CONN 01	ENGINEERING 01	MEDICINE 01

FOCUSES: Starfleet Command, Intelligence, Federation Law

STRESS: 11   **RESISTANCE:** 0

ATTACKS:
- Unarmed Strike (Melee, 4▲ Knockdown, Size 1H, Non-lethal)
- Phaser Type-2 (Ranged, 6▲, Size 1H, Charge)

SPECIAL RULES:
- **The Bigger Picture:** When Admiral Raner attempts a *Persuasion* Task and uses Threat to buy additional d20s, she may reroll one d20.
- **Menacing**

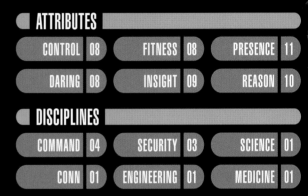

WARNING!
PROHIBITED
PHASE CLOAKING
MODIFICATIONS
INSTALLED

395876 329	65	1654
2359	54	5935
39685623 153	87	2469
436291	12	9571
39825 23091	20	2365
289385623 29	36	7653

57 85-3 **57** 57 87-4

28 78-1 **28** 28 12-2

6 95-5 **6** 6 53-6

34 42-1   34 43-2 **34** 34 45-7   34 46-3

56 47-7   58 83-8 **56** 58 31-9   57 74-1

STARFLEET INTELLIGENCE AGENT [NOTABLE NPC]

Intelligence agents are specialists within Starfleet, with proficiency in covert operations and espionage inside and outside the Federation. Their role in gathering information on threats to the Federation is invaluable, and several breakthroughs in criminal investigations and strategic planning have been credited to their actions. This includes stings on Orion smuggling operations, and intelligence on the Romulan Star Empire on the other side of the Neutral Zone.

TRAITS: Human, Cautious

VALUES:
- I Am the Unseen Hand of Starfleet

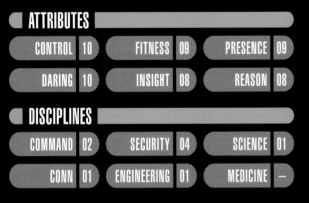

ATTRIBUTES

CONTROL	10	FITNESS	09	PRESENCE	09
DARING	10	INSIGHT	08	REASON	08

DISCIPLINES

COMMAND	02	SECURITY	04	SCIENCE	01
CONN	01	ENGINEERING	01	MEDICINE	—

FOCUSES: Undercover Operations, Espionage, Intelligence Analysis

STRESS: 13   **RESISTANCE:** 0 (4)

ATTACKS:
- Unarmed Strike (Melee, 5🡹 Knockdown, Size 1H, Non-lethal)
- Phaser Type-1 (Ranged, 6🡹, Size 1H, Charge, Hidden 1)

SPECIAL RULES:
- **Constantly Watching:** When the agent attempts a Task to detect danger or hidden enemies, reduce the Difficulty by 1.
- **Trained to Withstand Interrogation:** Whenever the agent attempts a Task to resist being intimidated or threatened, they add one d20 to their dice pool.
- **Menacing**

OTHER EQUIPMENT:
- **Escalation** Personal Force Field

LUTHER SLOAN [MAJOR NPC]

Luther Sloan is the supposed director of Section 31, the unrecognized covert department of Federation "dirty tricks". Little is known about his personal life, though hints about an early career in Starfleet Intelligence indicate how he ended up leading the Section 31 organization. Records, of course, can't corroborate any theory of his origin or profession.

Sloane is a calculating individual, who twists facts to suit his objectives or ambitions, but that's not to say he is selfishly driven. He is someone who must protect Federation citizens from a universe that doesn't share their sense of right and wrong, and his motivations seem to be the preservation of the Federation and its member species. His methods, however, are questionable. As the leader of Section 31 he's not scared to get his hands rather dirty in the line of duty.

TRAITS: Human, Covert Mastermind

VALUES:
- I Am a Man of Secrets
- The Ends Justify the Means
- A Prodigy of Starfleet Intelligence
- Breaking Federation Principles in Order to Keep It Safe

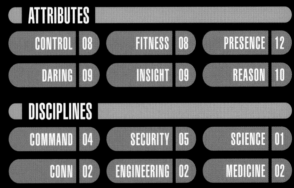

ATTRIBUTES

CONTROL	08	FITNESS	08	PRESENCE	12
DARING	09	INSIGHT	09	REASON	10

DISCIPLINES

COMMAND	04	SECURITY	05	SCIENCE	01
CONN	02	ENGINEERING	02	MEDICINE	02

FOCUSES: Espionage, Infiltration, Manipulation, Starfleet Security, Disguise, Interrogation

STRESS: 13   **RESISTANCE:** 0

ATTACKS:
- Unarmed Strike (Melee, 6🡹 Knockdown, Size 1H, Non-lethal)
- Phaser Type-2 (Ranged, 8🡹, Size 1H, Charge)

SPECIAL RULES:
- **Threatening 4**
- **Commission:** Sloan can counterfeit records to give himself a Starfleet commission or civilian rank (excluding flag officer ranks) and remove those records just as easily. Sloane may begin with a rank at the beginning of a mission for no cost. This counts as a Trait: "Counterfeit Commission 2" which increases the

Sloan, or Director Sloan, is an incredibly elusive individual. Many in Starfleet will never encounter the man, and a tiny number of people will work with him. His excellence lies in the manipulation of his targets: his recruitment methods test their characters, and only if they can begin to outsmart him does he consider bringing them under Section 31's wing.

UNKNOWING AGENTS

Sloan may find it easier and safer to manipulate the Player Characters from afar, influencing the missions they are assigned and nudging them in the right direction. This can be represented by the Gamemaster spending Threat for the unexpected to occur or through the actions of NPCs under Sloan's influence. There may even be a trail of breadcrumbs to follow showing Sloan's influence,

meaning the characters he is manipulating may be able to shed a little light on his clandestine organization.

PERSONAL RECRUITMENT

Sloan also oversees the personality tests he imposes on people who are being framed for security breaches and his possible agents. He's not above manipulating a target's sense of reality and putting them through grueling psychological tests to measure their character and ability to cope as a covert operative. He has abducted Starfleet personnel, convinced them of entirely false circumstances, and then resorted to blackmail. He will do whatever it takes to reach his ends, and could target an individual amongst the Players' crew.

Difficulty of its discovery by 2. To change or create a new rank requires 2 Threat during a mission.

- **Profiling:** Whenever Sloan attempts to intimidate or deceive a character with a *Persuasion* Task, he adds one d20 to his dice pool.
- **Counterintelligence:** When a Player uses the *Obtain Information* spend to enquire about Sloan, you may spend 1 Threat to choose whether to answer the question truthfully or mislead the Players. This tactic can also be used as a double bluff when revealing truthful information.
- **Lethal Implant:** By spending 1 Threat per Main Character in the scene, Sloan may activate a neural implant that kills him instantly to avoid exposing Section 31 or its operations.

INFORMANT [MINOR NPC]

Informants provide their Starfleet Intelligence contacts with intelligence on events, people and items with which they have close contact. These individuals can come from any walk of life, but often have a deep-seated appreciation for the Federation and its principals. This makes them valuable in the fight against moral corruption and external threats.

TRAITS: Alien (see below), Paranoid

ATTRIBUTES

CONTROL 07	FITNESS 08	PRESENCE 09
DARING 08	INSIGHT 10	REASON 09

DISCIPLINES

COMMAND –	SECURITY 02	SCIENCE –
CONN 02	ENGINEERING 01	MEDICINE 01

FOCUSES: (See below)

STRESS: 10   **RESISTANCE:** 0

ATTACKS:
- Unarmed Strike (Melee, 3⚔ Knockdown, Size 1H, Non-lethal)

SPECIAL RULES:
- **Species Focus:** The informant gains one Focus, equal to their species, as chosen by the Gamemaster. This Focus applies when they are trying to get information about someone of their own species.

9874321068 963 09840
7920 256 65408
966333 741 07895
32165 524 969
6219876954 369 1190
02498763 458 884
36936574 987 7962
287278241 321 41166
159517357 458 46882
798621 963 1089
9354477856 159 68712
58550322 753 556
06858756 852 21080
451554 050 LCARS

ACCESS DENIED

SYSTEMS

RESTRICTED INFORMATION

INSUFFICIENT SECURITY
LEVEL DETECTED

RANKING OFFICER INFORMED

PLEASE STAND BY FOR
FURTHER INSTRUCTION

MODE SELECT

7390-4504

LCARS

CONSOLE 26 ADGE

OPERATIONS PERSONNEL
STARFLEET CORPS OF ENGINEERS

CAPTAIN HERMAN ZIMMERMAN [MAJOR NPC]

Captain Zimmerman has had a long career commanding various starships but, most notably, he is a contributing design specialist for Shipyard Operations, and worked on the designs of the *Galaxy*- and *Defiant*-class starships, notably the *U.S.S. Enterprise*-D and the *U.S.S. Defiant.*

TRAITS: Human

VALUES:
- Design Moves Technology to its Preferred State
- Most Comfortable in the Center Chair

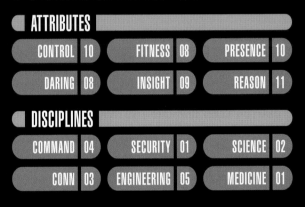

ATTRIBUTES

CONTROL	10	FITNESS	08	PRESENCE	10
DARING	08	INSIGHT	09	REASON	11

DISCIPLINES

COMMAND	04	SECURITY	01	SCIENCE	02
CONN	03	ENGINEERING	05	MEDICINE	01

FOCUSES: Structural Integrity Fields, Warp Field Dynamics, Weapon Array Configuration, Composure, Starship Tactics, Technological Innovation

STRESS: 9   **RESISTANCE:** 0

ATTACKS:
- Unarmed Strike (Melee, 2⚔ Knockdown, Size 1H, Non-lethal)
- Phaser Type-1 (Ranged, 3⚔, Size 1H, Charge, Hidden 1)

SPECIAL RULES:
- **Veteran Officer:** Should Captain Zimmerman ever spend Threat in place of Determination (see below), roll 1⚔. If an Effect is rolled, immediately regain the spent points of Threat.
- **Innovation:** If Captain Zimmerman is assisting a Main Character in developing a prototype piece of technology,

OVERVIEW

During their commissions, Starfleet officers will eventually meet and work alongside personnel from Starfleet Engineering. They may even be recruited into the department, and be assigned missions under an engineer. This section presents several Non-Player Characters from the Corps of Engineers that the Gamemaster can use in missions.

the Main Character or Zimmerman can reroll one d20 during Tasks to create that prototype.
- **A Little More Power:** When Zimmerman succeeds at an Engineering Task aboard a starship, Players may spend one Momentum to regain one spent Power (repeatable).
- **Starship Expert (Talent)**

ADMIRAL JOHN HARRIMAN [MAJOR NPC]

Admiral Harriman served as commanding officer of the *U.S.S. Enterprise*-B, in 2293. The events of its maiden voyage left a lasting impression on him with the loss of his childhood hero, James T. Kirk. He had a dedication plaque to Kirk made and installed in main engineering of the *Enterprise*-B. His missions quickly took him away from the bridge of the *Enterprise*, and he moved into more covert operations along the Romulan Neutral Zone. After almost resigning his commission in 2311, he was promoted to Admiral, and this eventually led to his role as Starfleet Corps of Engineers Command Liaison in the 2360s and after. He coordinates the efforts of the Engineer Corps with Starfleet Command itself, assigning personnel and equipment throughout Starfleet. Unlike some more formal Admirals, Harriman recognizes potential and welcomes questions and opinions in many of his meetings with Starfleet personnel.

TRAITS: Human, Elderly, Flag Officer

VALUES:
- Starfleet is a Family Tradition
- Keeping an Old Admiral Busy
- Risk is Part of the Game if You Want the Captain's Chair

FLAG OFFICERS IN PLAY

FLAG OFFICER VALUES

Each flag officer NPC has several Values that work in the same was as for other NPCs, adding to or removing from Threat rather than generating and spending Determination. In situations where a flag officer is an important part of a mission and taking an active part, the flag officer NPC's Values can have additional importance.

At any point during a mission, a flag officer NPC may select one of their Values and add it to the list of Directives currently in play for that mission. This reflects the impact of the flag officer's beliefs and inclinations on their command style. Should this Directive be Challenged, this may change the way that the flag officer views any challenging Character, possibly creating a rival or adversary.

THREAT AND ALLIED NPCS

Some flag officer NPCs have the Menacing or Threatening special rules. In play, a flag officer may be an ally or antagonist depending on context. It is common for admirals to get into heated debates with command officers, but they all remain Starfleet. In such situations extra thought is needed for these special abilities, given that NPC interactions with Threat differ depending on whether they are friend or foe.

MENACING

This ability adds one point to Threat when the character enters the scene. The NPC can be an ally or an adversary. Always add one Threat. This isn't always due to the character, but can reflect the circumstances that need an admiral's involvement. A flag officer taking an interest means the mission is especially important, dangerous or sensitive.

THREATENING X

This provides the character with a number of Threat, to be spent exclusively by that character, rather than from the group pool. As NPCs allied to Player Characters add to Threat, rather than spending from it, there is another consideration. When a character with Threatening X is opposed to the Player Characters, points from their personal Threat pool can be spent instead of points from the main Threat pool. When a character with Threatening X is aligned with the Player Characters, points from the NPC's personal Threat pool can be spent instead of adding points to the main Threat pool. This reflects the character's control over a situation. Flag officers are better able than most to keep a situation from escalating or maintain the pressure if required.

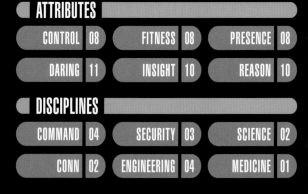

ATTRIBUTES

CONTROL 08	FITNESS 08	PRESENCE 08
DARING 11	INSIGHT 10	REASON 10

DISCIPLINES

COMMAND 04	SECURITY 03	SCIENCE 02
CONN 02	ENGINEERING 04	MEDICINE 01

FOCUSES: Romulan Star Empire, Espionage, Quantum Singularity Technology, Sabotage, Personnel Management, Hand Phasers

STRESS: 11   **RESISTANCE:** 0

ATTACKS:
- Unarmed Strike (Melee, 4⬟ Knockdown, Size 1H, Non-lethal)
- Phaser Type-1 (Ranged, 5⬟, Size 1H, Charge, Hidden 1)

SPECIAL RULES:
- **Sabotage:** Admiral Harriman adds one d20 to his dice pool when attempting Engineering Tasks related to sabotaging equipment.
- **Menacing**
- **Dauntless (Talent)**
- **Advisor (Talent)**

DOCTOR LEAH BRAHMS [NOTABLE NPC]

Dr. Brahms is a key designer of the propulsion systems of the *Galaxy* and *Nebula*-class starships at the Utopia Planitia Fleet Yards. A graduate of the Daystrom Institute of Technology, she has a brilliant mind for the theory of propulsion and subspace designs.

TRAITS: Human

VALUES:
- More Comfortable with Engine Schematics than People

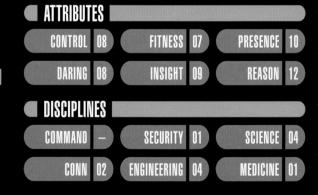

ATTRIBUTES

CONTROL 08	FITNESS 07	PRESENCE 10
DARING 08	INSIGHT 09	REASON 12

DISCIPLINES

COMMAND –	SECURITY 01	SCIENCE 04
CONN 02	ENGINEERING 04	MEDICINE 01

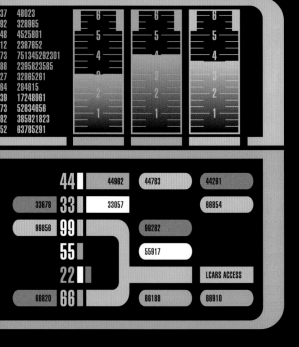

FOCUSES: Impulse Drive, Warp Field Dynamics, Subspace Physics

STRESS: 8   RESISTANCE: 0

ATTACKS:
- Unarmed Strike (Melee, 2▲ Knockdown, Size 1H, Non-lethal)

SPECIAL RULES:
- **All Theory:** Players who are engaging in technological innovation may use Dr. Brahms' papers to gain assistance on their Engineering or Science Tasks using Dr. Brahms' own Attribute + Discipline combination if, and only if, the innovation relates to one of her Focuses.
- **Extraordinary Reason 1**
- **Procedural Compliance (Talent)**

LEAH BRAHMS IN PLAY

Dr. Leah Brahms is, at her core, a professional woman. She can be almost Vulcan in her tact when it comes to engineering and theoretical discussion, but her brilliant mind shines through while working. She doesn't suffer fools at all let along gladly, and is clear and concise of her expectations of the Starfleet Engineers who work with engines she has designed.

COMMANDER MAHMUD AL-KHALED [NOTABLE NPC]

Lt. Commander Al-Khaled is a well-regarded repair specialist, and eventually Command Liaison in the Corps of Engineers in 2280. He had command of the *U.S.S. Aephas*, a *Miranda*-class starship during his field work before he lead the Corps at the Tucker Memorial Building in Starfleet Command HQ. Mahmud is passionate about his work, insisting that the efficiency of the personnel under his guidance is of the highest standard.

TRAITS: Human

VALUES:
- To Achieve High Standards, You Must Expect High Standards

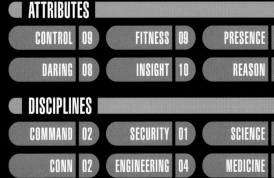

ATTRIBUTES

| CONTROL | 09 | FITNESS | 09 | PRESENCE | 08 |
| DARING | 08 | INSIGHT | 10 | REASON | 10 |

DISCIPLINES

| COMMAND | 02 | SECURITY | 01 | SCIENCE | 01 |
| CONN | 02 | ENGINEERING | 04 | MEDICINE | 01 |

FOCUSES: Starship Repair, Warp Core Maintenance, Ground Vehicles

STRESS: 10   RESISTANCE: 0

ATTACKS:
- Unarmed Strike (Melee, 2▲ Knockdown, Size 1H, Non-lethal)
- Phaser Type-1 (Ranged, 3▲, Size 1H, Charge, Hidden 1)

SPECIAL RULES:
- **I Know Starfleet Ships:** Whenever Commander Al-Khaled attempts a Task to determine the source of a technical problem aboard a starship with the "Federation" Trait, add one bonus d20.
- **My Repairs Do the Talking:** Whenever Al-Khaled attempts a Task using Presence to direct an engineering team, he may use Engineering instead of Command.

OPERATIONS PERSONNEL
STARFLEET PERSONNEL

OVERVIEW

The Notable and Minor NPCs in this section are generic, allowing the Gamemaster to adjust them for different situations. This allows these characters to be used as people from Federation worlds or other civilizations, depending on the needs of the game.

Here the NPCs are listed as human, and Attributes have been increased due to their species (in the case of humans, any three.) To change the character's species, change the character's species Trait, reduce the three highest Attributes by one each, and then apply the new species' Attribute modifiers. It may also be appropriate to change the character's Values, adjust Focuses to suit the chosen culture, or add any appropriate Talents or special rules for the species.

QUARTERMASTER [NOTABLE NPC]

The quartermaster was a highly visible and important position in the 22nd Century era of Starfleet. Quartermasters can still be found on the occasional Starfleet installation, and are responsible for the distribution and allocation of supplies and resources. They can requisition supplies and equipment from Fleet Operations, and are a department head's point of contact for requesting gear for their team.

TRAITS: Human

VALUE: Fail to Prepare and You Prepare to Fail

ATTRIBUTES

CONTROL 09	FITNESS 08	PRESENCE 10
DARING 08	INSIGHT 10	REASON 09

DISCIPLINES

COMMAND 02	SECURITY 01	SCIENCE 02
CONN 01	ENGINEERING 03	MEDICINE 01

FOCUSES: Resources Management, Repair Procedures

STRESS: 9   **RESISTANCE:** 0

ATTACKS:
- Unarmed Strike (Melee, 2▲ Knockdown, Size 1H, Non-lethal)
- Phaser Type-1 (Ranged, 3▲, Size 1H, Charge, Hidden 1)

SPECIAL RULES:
- **Requisitions:** Whenever the quartermaster assists Main Characters in creating an Advantage by supplying equipment they may reroll their d20.
- **Contacts in Fleet Ops:** Whenever the quartermaster is attempting a *Persuasion* Task to request resources from Starfleet Command, they may add 1d20 to their dice pool.

TRANSPORTER CHIEF [NOTABLE NPC]

Transporter chiefs are key personnel aboard Starfleet installations and ships, and report to the chief of operations. They monitor and coordinate energy-matter-scrambler transportation of personnel and cargo, often in person from a transporter room or cargo bay. They are usually a petty officer, ensign or lieutenant aboard Starfleet ships and stations.

TRAITS: Human

VALUE: Are You Sure These Are the Right Coordinates?

ATTRIBUTES

CONTROL	11	FITNESS	08	PRESENCE	08
DARING	08	INSIGHT	10	REASON	09

DISCIPLINES

COMMAND	01	SECURITY	02	SCIENCE	02
CONN	01	ENGINEERING	03	MEDICINE	01

FOCUSES: Transporters, Containment Procedures

STRESS: 10   **RESISTANCE:** 0

ATTACKS:
- Unarmed Strike (Melee, 3▲ Knockdown, Size 1H, Non-lethal)
- Phaser Type-1 (Ranged, 4▲, Size 1H, Charge, Hidden 1)

SPECIAL RULES:
- **Technical Expertise:** Whenever the transporter chief is assisted by the ship's Computers or Sensors, they may reroll one d20 (which may be the ship's die).
- **Emergency Transport:** Whenever the transporter chief attempts a transport using Daring instead of Control, they may reduce the Difficulty by 1, to a minimum of 1.

ENGINEERING SPECIALIST [MINOR NPC]

An engineering specialist, or systems engineer, is a Starfleet engineer with a particular Focus. These individuals are often brought aboard a starship or starbase to facilitate repairs or upgrades in a particular area, such as the warp fields, computing, replicators and transporters, phasers, or torpedo technology. Their knowledge often strays into the theoretical too, and commissioned Starfleet officers who are deemed "specialists" are often pioneers in their own field of expertise.

TRAITS: Human

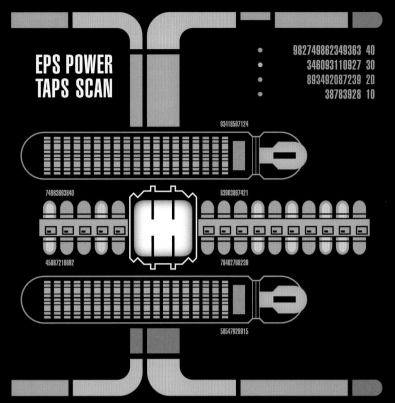

EPS POWER TAPS SCAN

- 982749862349363 40
- 346093110927 30
- 893492087239 20
- 38783928 10

ATTRIBUTES

CONTROL	10	FITNESS	08	PRESENCE	07
DARING	08	INSIGHT	09	REASON	10

DISCIPLINES

COMMAND	01	SECURITY	01	SCIENCE	02
CONN	01	ENGINEERING	02	MEDICINE	01

FOCUSES: *See Special Rules, below*

STRESS: 9   **RESISTANCE:** 0

ATTACKS:
- Unarmed Strike (Melee, 2▲ Knockdown, Size 1H, Non-lethal)
- Phaser Type-1 (Ranged, 3▲, Size 1H, Charge, Hidden 1)

SPECIAL RULES:
- **Field of Expertise:** The engineering specialist gains a Focus in one of the following fields of engineering, and while attempting a Task in which it applies, adds 1d20 to their dice pool.
  - Warp fields
  - Electro-plasma power systems
  - Structural integrity fields
  - Energy-matter-scrambler technology
  - Quantum mechanics

COMMUNICATIONS OFFICER [NOTABLE NPC]

The communications officer was a separate bridge position until the late 23rd Century. These operations staff were responsible for ship-wide, local and long-distance (subspace) communications. Early in Starfleet history, before the proliferation of the universal translator, communications officers were required to be fluent in several Federation languages, and have a familiarity with other key languages such as Klingon.

TRAITS: Human

VALUE: Language Is the Key to Exploring New Civilizations

ATTRIBUTES

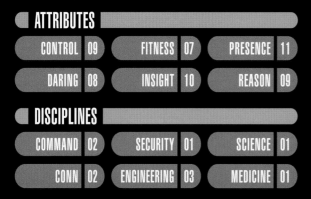

CONTROL 09	FITNESS 07	PRESENCE 11
DARING 08	INSIGHT 10	REASON 09

DISCIPLINES

COMMAND 02	SECURITY 01	SCIENCE 01
CONN 02	ENGINEERING 03	MEDICINE 01

FOCUSES: Alien Languages, Translation

STRESS: 8   **RESISTANCE:** 0

ATTACKS:
- Unarmed Strike (Melee, 2▲ Knockdown, Size 1H, Non-lethal)
- Phaser Type-1 (Ranged, 3▲, Size 1H, Charge, Hidden 1)

SPECIAL RULES:
- **Cautious (Engineering):** Whenever the communications officer attempts a Task with Engineering, and buys additional dice with Momentum, they may reroll one d20.
- **Interpretive Translation:** The communications officer may always choose to Succeed at Cost when attempting to translate a language with which they are unfamiliar. The Complication limits what they understand to the most basic version of the message.

OPERATIONS OFFICER [NOTABLE NPC]

The operations officer, at the bridge ops station, is the head of ship operations. The two bridge positions of communications and science officer were amalgamated into this role in the 24th Century. These officers must be familiar with both the Science and Engineering Disciplines. They interpret key data and act on the orders of the commanding officers aboard a ship maintaining communication, scanning and other operational duties.

TRAITS: Human

VALUE: From This Chair I Am in Control

ATTRIBUTES

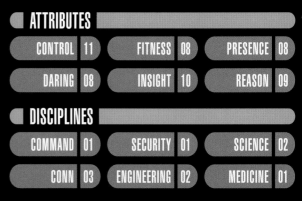

CONTROL 11	FITNESS 08	PRESENCE 08
DARING 08	INSIGHT 10	REASON 09

DISCIPLINES

COMMAND 01	SECURITY 01	SCIENCE 02
CONN 03	ENGINEERING 02	MEDICINE 01

FOCUSES: Sensor Operations, Starfleet Reporting Procedures

STRESS: 9   **RESISTANCE:** 0

ATTACKS:
- Unarmed Strike (Melee, 2▲ Knockdown, Size 1H, Non-lethal)
- Phaser Type-1 (Ranged, 3▲, Size 1H, Charge, Hidden 1)

SPECIAL RULES:
- **Operational Oversight:** Whenever the operations officer attempts a Task of another station or department, they ignore any increase in Difficulty due to their oversight role as operations officer.

REPAIR TEAM LEADER [NOTABLE NPC]

Often members of the Corps of Engineers when in space dock, and officers in the engineering division aboard a starship, repair team leaders lead groups of engineers. They restore systems from serious damage aboard Starfleet vessels and, when in combat or a crisis, damage control teams will be sent out to keep systems online. It is their job to fight fires, both literally and metaphorically. In space dock, these repair teams work long hours to help maintain, upgrade and otherwise repair ships on the frontline of Federation space.

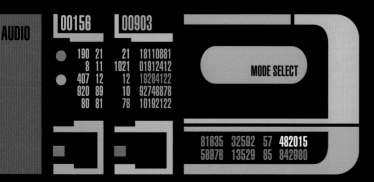

ATTRIBUTES

CONTROL 10	FITNESS 10	PRESENCE 07
DARING 10	INSIGHT 09	REASON 08

DISCIPLINES

COMMAND 01	SECURITY 01	SCIENCE 02
CONN 02	ENGINEERING 03	MEDICINE 01

ATTACKS:

- Unarmed Strike (Melee, 2▲ Knockdown, Size 1H, Non-lethal)
- Phaser Type-1 (Ranged, 3▲, Size 1H, Charge, Hidden 1)

SPECIAL RULES:

- **Pushing the Deadline:** Whenever the repair team leader succeeds at an Engineering or Science Task as part of a Timed Challenge or Extended Task, they may halve the number of time intervals taken by spending 1 Momentum.

OPERATIONS PERSONNEL
SUPPORTING CHARACTERS

STARFLEET SECURITY OFFICER

This character is a specialist in internal security aboard Starfleet installations and colonies, and is expected to safeguard visitors, dignitaries, and keep the peace aboard a Starfleet vessel. They are often responsible for the custody of prisoners, and are seen escorting persons to the brig or standing guard over their cell. They also escort senior officers on away missions, often securing an area before other personnel beam into an unsecure location.

ATTRIBUTES

CONTROL 10	FITNESS 09	PRESENCE 08
DARING 09	INSIGHT 08	REASON 07

DISCIPLINES

COMMAND 02	SECURITY 04	SCIENCE 01
CONN 01	ENGINEERING 02	MEDICINE 03

OVERVIEW

This section provides a varied selection of interesting supporting characters that can be introduced during an ongoing game specialized in Engineering or Security.

They are all built using the *Supporting Characters* rules on page 134 of the **Star Trek Adventures** core rulebook. Each one is accompanied by notes on how that character might be customized when reintroduced in later missions.

None of the supporting characters include character species effects. In cases where a different species is needed, add a Trait related to the character's species, and increase the character's Attributes accordingly. The most straightforward option is to use Human as the default character species, adding the Trait "Human", and increasing any three Attributes by +1.

FOCUSES: Internal Security, Hand Phasers, Squad Tactics

STRESS: 13 **RESISTANCE:** 0

ATTACKS:

- Unarmed Strike (Melee, 5▲ Knockdown, Size 1H, Non-lethal)
- Phaser Type-2 (Ranged, 7▲, Size 1H, Charge)
- Escalation Phaser Type-3 (Ranged, 8▲, Size 2H, Accurate, Charge)

USE AND DEVELOPMENT

Security officers are often deployed to bolster away missions, or in teams of their own aboard a starship to maintain security or repel boarding parties. Commanding officer main characters may requisition security officers up to a full team, while the chief of security will often use Crew Support to give themselves an individual officer or team of security personnel.

- **Species :** Aside from humans, Andorians, Bajorans, and Tellarites are all good choices for security personnel, with excellent Control for phaser fights or Daring for melee attacks.

- **Rank:** The character will probably be an Ensign, Lieutenant (junior grade) or even a non-commissioned officer.

- **Values:** A Value that helps the character during combat, such as overcoming physical adversity, can be useful. The character does need to have another way to gain Determination, such as being given it by a Commanding Officer, or a second Value that can generate complications.

- **Attributes:** Insight (tactical vigilance), Control (marksmanship), or Daring (melee combat) are all useful Attributes to increase.

- **Disciplines:** Security is the discipline to increase, but Command (leading a team) and Engineering (disabling security systems, or repairing equipment) are useful too.

- **Focuses:** Additional Focuses can give the character a broad skill base and allow them to engage in a range of situations. Focuses like *Martial Arts* or *Federation Law* can enhance the character's success.

- **Talents:** In a support role, *Close Protection* and *Pack Tactics* are excellent choices for security personnel being led by a Main Character.

STARFLEET ENGINEER'S MATE

An engineer's mate is slang derived from the actual engineering position held aboard ships in the 23rd Century and much earlier. An engineer's mate is an assistant, formally the assistant chief engineer, who helps the chief with their day-to-day duties. They're often a sounding board for ideas and a source of theories; they oversee routine maintenance, and lead teams of engineers in the chief's name.

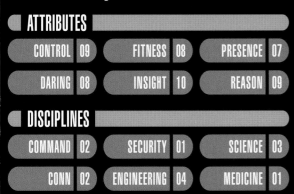

ATTRIBUTES

CONTROL 09	FITNESS 08	PRESENCE 07
DARING 08	INSIGHT 10	REASON 09

DISCIPLINES

COMMAND 02	SECURITY 01	SCIENCE 03
CONN 02	ENGINEERING 04	MEDICINE 01

FOCUSES: Warp Drive, Electro-Plasma Systems, Quick-Fixes

STRESS: 9   **RESISTANCE:** 0

ATTACKS:
- Unarmed Strike (Melee, 2▲ Knockdown, Size 1H, Non-lethal)
- Phaser Type-1 (Ranged, 3▲, Size 1H, Charge, Hidden 1)

USE AND DEVELOPMENT

Engineer's mates are brought into scenes as direct assistants to the chief engineer, or they represent a coordinated team attempting adaptations, repairs or projects aboard the ship or planet side.

- **Species:** Aside from Humans, most species make fine engineers, however Denobulans, Tellarites, Xindi-Arboreal, and Zakdorn excel.

- **Rank:** The character will probably be an Ensign, Lieutenant or a senior non-commissioned rank.

- **Values:** Values that focus the mind and drive the character forward when facing problems or unexplained situations, or when striving for solutions to technical problems, work the best for engineering supporting characters.

- **Attributes:** Many Attributes are used by Engineers, so a broad increase would work best for these characters, notably Control, Daring, Insight, and Reason when working and, perhaps, Presence when leading a team.

- **Disciplines:** With Engineering already at 4, it may be better if Science or Conn is increased for this character

to enhance their ability and understanding of the theoretical underpinning of sub-space, faster-than-light flight and Starfleet technology generally.

- **Focuses:** Additional Focuses can give the character a broad mix of expertise, enabling them to successfully repair many different kinds of equipment. Focuses like *Biomechanics, Impulse Drives, Structural Integrity, Computers, Robotics* or *Deflector Technology* would give them a wider knowledge base.

- **Talents:** Any Engineering Talent, like *A Little More Power, I Know My Ship,* and *Jury-Rig* are excellent choices for the Supporting Character to assist their successful Tasks.

MACO SOLDIER

Military Assault Command Operations was a 22nd Century United Earth organization formed as a military defensive/security force. All MACO troops attended West Point Military Academy in New York, North America. They provided security services aboard the *Enterprise NX-01* on its mission, proving crucial to its success in several skirmishes and battles against the Xindi between 2153–54.

A "may-ko" soldier was well equipped, even ahead of their Starfleet comrades, with armor and weapons at the cutting edge of United Earth technology and design.

TRAITS: Human

ATTRIBUTES

CONTROL 10	FITNESS 11	PRESENCE 08
DARING 09	INSIGHT 08	REASON 08

DISCIPLINES

COMMAND 03	SECURITY 04	SCIENCE 01
CONN 01	ENGINEERING 02	MEDICINE 02

FOCUSES: Survival, Marksmanship, Squad Tactics

STRESS: 15   **RESISTANCE:** 2

ATTACKS:
- Stun Baton (Melee, 5▲ Intense, Size 1H, Non-lethal)
- Phase Pistol (Ranged, 7▲, Size 1H)
- Particle Rifle (Ranged, 8▲, Size 2H, Accurate)
- **Escalation** Stun Grenade (Ranged, 7▲ Area, Size 1H, Grenade, Non-lethal)

USE AND DEVELOPMENT

MACOs are deployed to protect United Earth assets, whether that be personnel, vessels or installations. Their presence can be threatening to others, as their equipment is an overtly military presence than being diplomatic or exploratory. As such, whenever a MACO Supporting Character or team is introduced using Crew Support **they also cost 1 Threat as per the Escalation rules.**

- **Species:** MACOs are always Human, and this has been included in the Attributes above.

- **Rank:** MACOs have their own rank structure, from private, to corporal (in charge of a fireteam), sergeant (in charge of a squad or section) and major (in charge of a platoon or company of MACOs).

- **Values:** A Value that helps the character protect the fellow Humans, related to discipline and battle readiness, works well. The character does need to have another way to gain Determination, such as being given it by a Commanding Officer, or a second Value that can generate complications.

- **Attributes:** Control (for ranged accuracy), Daring (for quick thinking and bravery), or Fitness (for additional Stress) are all Attributes that would enhance the MACO.

- **Disciplines:** Security may be an obvious Attribute to increase, however Command or Medicine may be other options depending on how the supporting character's specific role is fleshed out.

- **Focuses :** Additional Focuses should give the character more intensive training, like *Stamina*, *Explosives*, *Combat First Aid,* or *Personal Protection* depending on their duty.

- **Talents:** As military personnel, *Quick to Action, Pack Tactics,* or *Follow My Lead* would be relevant Talents to give a MACO added capability in conflict scenarios.

584572980200 29845	07.10	RULES OF PLAY	098
	07.20	STARTING A GAME	106
	07.30	THE BATTLEFIELD	108
	07.40	WEAPONS AND EQUIPMENT	109
	07.50	MISSIONS	113
	07.60	TOKENS	117

RED ALERT
RULES OF PLAY

"WAR ISN'T A GOOD LIFE, BUT IT'S LIFE."

— CAPTAIN JAMES T. KIRK

With *Star Trek Adventures: Red Alert*, your gaming group can add an exciting three-dimensional tactical experience to your RPG encounters. Now, Federation away teams can do battle against Klingon warriors, Romulan strike teams, Borg drones, or any number of other threats on far-flung worlds across the Galaxy. Whether you're a seasoned veteran of tabletop campaigns or a fresh-from-the-academy redshirt, you'll soon be controlling your own away team and battling over the fate of worlds or the entire Galaxy!

These rules will be familiar to existing players, but are straightforward enough for new players to understand quickly. *Star Trek Adventures: Red Alert* can be used as an exciting substitute for combat encounters in your roleplaying sessions, or a way of setting up quick combat encounters using your collection of *Star Trek Adventures* miniatures.

THE MOST IMPORTANT RULE

It's nearly impossible for a set of rules to cover every conceivable situation that could arise during a game. Disputes over rules should always be resolved in a spirit of cooperation and sportsmanship. Ultimately, if no agreement can be reached, we recommend that players each roll a D20, dicing off until there is a clear winner: the player with highest score is right this time around. Remember, the aim of the game is to have fun in a friendly, competitive spirit, and that means letting your opponent have fun too! Settling differences in a friendly manner is paramount to having fun, so this could be called the most important rule in the game!

THINGS YOU'LL NEED

Before you can play your first mission, there are a few things you should gather in preparation. Obviously, the most important part of the game is the miniatures themselves. In addition, however, you will need:

BATTLEFIELD

Red Alert combat encounters are played with the **Star Trek Adventures** Tile Sets available from Modiphius. These sets represent the environments for the scenarios, and are divided into the zones required for play. They are fully rendered with top-down scenery walls and obstacles.

DICE

You will need a handful of **twenty-sided dice** (referred to as D20) to play this game, along with some special six-sided **Challenge Dice**. *(See sidebar.)*

TOKENS

Red Alert uses a number of Momentum and Threat tokens, in a similar way to the main **Star Trek Adventures** rules. You'll need one set of tokens to track Momentum for the two sides; one uses the blue Momentum tokens, the other uses the red Threat tokens.

MARKERS

You'll also need a set of markers, provided for you in the back of this supplement.

BASIC PRINCIPLES

The pages that follow present the game rules in the order they are needed in play. There are a few basic terms and principles that need to be introduced right from the start. These are rules and terminology that affect every aspect of the game.

MODELS

The miniatures used to play **Star Trek: Red Alert** are also referred to as "models"; the two terms can be considered interchangeable. The models under your control represents your crew, such as a Federation away team or Klingon war band.

In game terms your crew is split into several **units** which are either activated individually as **characters** or are grouped into **squads**.

CHARACTERS

Characters are individuals whose skills and qualities outstrip that of a regular field agent or soldier. They are always fielded alone as a unit of one model.

SQUADS

Squads are a single unit comprising between two and ten models that act and fight together. For the purposes of Turns and actions squads count as a single unit. Even though there are many models in a squad, they can only normally attempt one Minor Action and one Task per Turn, and you roll one pool of dice for the whole squad as a unit.

CHALLENGE DICE

Challenge Dice are custom six-sided dice that have both damage values and special Effect symbols, denoted in the rules by the ▲ symbol.

If you don't have special Challenge Dice available, you can use normal six-sided dice instead; treat any die which rolls a 3 or 4 as blank, and any die which rolls a 5 or 6 as 1 damage, and an Effect.

CHALLENGE DICE RESULT TABLE

D6 RESULT	CHALLENGE DICE RESULT
1	1
2	2
3	0
4	0
5	1, plus Damage Effect
6	1, plus Damage Effect

Most **Star Trek Adventures: Red Alert** models are humanoid or human-sized, and are at around 32mm tall). Small size differences between these miniatures don't matter in game terms, although it does make them more realistic as models. This is why they are considered to be a standard size, unless it is specifically noted in a model's profile that this is not the case.

PROFILES

All models in the game have a **profile**. This is a set of characteristics and abilities defined in terms of numbers and special rules. These will be familiar to existing 2D20 system players!

There are six **Attributes** (Control, Daring, Fitness, Insight, Presence, and Reason), and six **Disciplines** (Command, Conn, Security, Engineering, Science, and Medicine). Profiles can be found in the **Star Trek Adventures** core rulebook, Chapter 11: Aliens and Adversaries (p.314), and in other supplements and sourcebooks.

ATTRIBUTES

- **Control** is about precision, accuracy, and careful timing. Control is used for ranged attacks.

- **Daring** comes into play whenever a character reacts to a new situation without doubt, hesitation, or caution. Daring is used for melee attacks.

- **Fitness** is about enduring hardship and employing force. It covers physical conditioning, general health and wellbeing, fortitude, and endurance. Fitness is used to measure Stress.

- **Insight** is about understanding people and their feelings, or being conscious of wisdom and learned experience. Insight can be used for certain objective Tasks.

- **Presence** is a person's ability to persuade or influence others, their natural charisma, and their ability to inspire and gain respect. Presence is used for certain objective Tasks.

- **Reason** reflects the mental aptitude of a character, problem-solving skills and logical thought processes. Reason can be used for certain objective Tasks.

DISCIPLINES

- **Command** covers a wide range of interpersonal interactions especially leadership, negotiation, and coordinating and motivating other people. Command is used to determine Initiative.

- **Conn** covers all piloting and ship operations. It is used for certain objective Tasks.

- **Security** is the use of force during combat for making attacks, as well as observing and analyzing threatening situations, and watching for potential perils. Security is used to increase the Challenge Dice rolled on a unit's attacks.

- **Engineering** governs understanding, repairing and designing technology. It is used for certain objective Tasks.

- **Medicine** is the understanding of the physical and mental makeup of life-forms, including the ailments and diseases that might befall them. Medicine is used with Daring to heal units.

FOCUSES

Focuses provide a specialty for a unit, representing specific knowledge or experience in a narrow field of expertise. To gain the benefit from a Focus, the unit needs to be attempting a related Task. For example, if a Klingon veteran is attempting a melee attack Task their "Hand-to-Hand" Focus applies. If a Focus applies to the Task, any d20 that rolls equal to or lower than the **Discipline** used, that die scores 2 successes.

The following Focuses apply to the Tasks below:

- **Melee attacks:** Hand-to-Hand; any named melee weapons; any named martial art.

- **Ranged attacks:** Any named ranged weapon.

- **Objective Tasks:** Any relevant Focus to the nature of the Task.

Ignore all other Focuses for the purposes of Star Trek Adventures: Red Alert.

TALENTS

Talents provide rules exceptions for characters or squads as listed in their profile. They apply so long as the conditions in the Talent description fit the actions and Tasks being undertaken.

DERIVED STATISTICS

STRESS

A unit's Stress points represent its current state of health. Stress is the sum of the unit's **Fitness + Security.** If a unit's Stress reaches 0, the unit is Injured, and removed from play.

RESISTANCE

Units with a measure of Resistance are hard to damage, due to their physical size, thick hide or personal armor. A Resistance value is deducted from damage inflicted against the model.

WEAPON DAMAGE

A unit's attack damage is a number of Challenge Dice (Λ) equal to the weapon's Λ rating + the unit's Security Discipline.

TASKS

Most important actions performed by models in *Red Alert* take the form of Tasks (*Star Trek Adventures* core rulebook p.77), and involve rolling a minimum of 2d20s in order to check for the Task's success or failure. All Tasks have a numeric **Target Number**, usually determined by adding together a specified Attribute and a Discipline (for example, a ranged attack uses the **Control** Attribute and the **Security** Discipline). For each D20 that scores equal to or less than the Target Number, one success is scored.

All Tasks also have a numeric **Difficulty** rating (for example, the base Difficulty of a ranged attack is 2, although this can vary depending on battlefield conditions). **If the number of successes scored equals or exceeds the Difficulty of the Task, then the Task is completed successfully**. If the number of successes is less than the Difficulty of the Task, then the Task attempt has failed.

OPPOSED TASKS

Sometimes, a unit will be required to make an Opposed Task roll against another unit. This represents one unit trying to perform an action that the other wishes to actively prevent. The main example of this is a melee attack.

The unit performing the Task is called the 'active' unit. The opposing unit is called the 'reactive' unit. Both units attempt a Task, as described above, each with their own Difficulty.

- If the active unit succeeds and scores more Momentum than the reactive unit, the Task is successful.

- If the active unit fails, or succeeds but scores equal to or fewer successes than the reactive unit, the Task is unsuccessful. (Reactive model breaks ties.)

- The player with the most successes reduces their Momentum gained by any Momentum their opponent gained, and keeps any remaining Momentum, to spend or save (see Momentum below.)

OBJECTIVE TASKS

Objective Tasks are Tasks that must be carried out by a character or squad during a game in order to win the game. They will usually require a Task, and may also need a character or squad to be carrying a particular item. These are defined in the scenario description.

TASK EXAMPLE

It's Jon's turn, and his Commander Riker (a unit on his own) is firing his phaser at a Klingon warrior. This is a **Control + Security Task** with a Difficulty of 2.

- Jon rolls 2d20, by default, and is looking to score **15 or under** on each dice to score a success. He scores a 12 and a 5, which gives him the 2 successes he needs.

OPPOSED TASK EXAMPLE

Jon's unit is attacking one belonging to James in close combat. As this is a melee attack, Jon and James both roll, in an Opposed Task. This is a **Daring + Security Task** with a Difficulty of 1.

- Jon's Target Number is 13, while James' Target number is 11. They both roll 2d20.

- Jon scores a 10 and a 7. James scores an 8 and a 16.

- Both Jon's and James' units have succeeded, but Jon gained 1 Momentum (by scoring 2 successes when only 1 was needed), and succeeds in attacking James' unit.

- James didn't gain any Momentum points from that roll, so Jon keeps the 1 Momentum he gained, and saves it.

HAND PHASERS

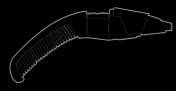

PHASER TYPE-1   PHASER TYPE-2

SCHEMATICS

MOMENTUM

Whenever a unit scores more successes than it needs, it generates Momentum. Momentum is a currency of points that can be used to improve successes or improve the odds of succeeding in future Tasks. When Momentum is generated, the Player has a choice: use the Momentum to improve that success or bank it for future use. A maximum pool of 6 Momentum can be banked by each Player.

SPENDING MOMENTUM

Momentum can either be spent to improve the success of the Task that has just been attempted, or it can be spent immediately before a Task is attempted. Certain Momentum Spends can only be done once; otherwise Momentum Spends are **Repeatable**, in which case there is no limit to how many times a Player can use Momentum Spends on a Task, unless otherwise stated.

CREATE OPPORTUNITY

The most common way to spend Momentum is to Create Opportunity, which grants extra d20 to roll before attempting a Task. The Difficulty of Tasks can go up to 5, which is impossible to reach on 2d20, so buying more dice grants more of a chance of success. Create Opportunity is an Immediate, Repeatable Momentum Spend, but it's cost escalates as below:

- +1d20 costs 1 Momentum
- +2d20 costs 3 Momentum
- +3d20 costs 6 Momentum

A Player may only ever roll a maximum of 5d20 for a Task.

CONFLICT MOMENTUM SPENDS

Characters may also spend Momentum as shown on the table below.

GIVING AN OPPONENT MOMENTUM

Players may give an opponent Momentum instead of spending their own, even if they have none saved. This means Momentum spends are always available to a Player, whether they have their own Momentum saved or not.

Only a maximum of 2 Momentum can be given to an opposing player, per Turn. Momentum given by an opponent cannot be spent immediately, and becomes available in their next turn.

A PLAYER'S TURN

Starting with the player with Initiative, Players take it in Turns to **activate one squad or a single character**, performing a minor action and a Task as they wish with that unit, and then handing play to the next player to do the same. Play continues in this "alternate activation" sequence until all Squads and Characters able to activate have done so.

Once activated, **a unit may perform one minor action, and one Task, in that order**. Models do not have to perform both, but if they perform a Task, they cannot perform a minor action afterwards. Once a unit has been activated, it cannot be activated again until all units have taken a Turn and a new Round begins.

MOVEMENT

When a Move minor action is taken, the unit moves to an adjacent zone. All members of a Squad must move together into the same zone, and occupy the same zone. If a Squad ever finds itself split across several zones for any reason, the Squad must perform the Move minor action to move the "stragglers" into the same zone as the rest of the unit.

A unit may move into a zone occupied by enemies, but may not move through that zone into another, or leave that zone (unless they are performing a Retreat Task).

ZONES AND BOUNDARIES

Every tile is divided into a number of zones delineated by grey lines. These represent the internal rooms, corridors and doorways of a location. A city street, for example, may divide zones around features like parked vehicles, the front of buildings, alleyways, and so forth. A relatively simple battlefield may consist of three to five significant zones, while complex environments may have many more, and have no fixed size.

MOMENTUM SPENDS

SPEND	COST	EFFECT
Create Opportunity	1+ (Immediate, Repeatable)	Buy extra d20 to roll before attempting a Task. The first die bought costs 1, the second die bought costs 2, the third die bought costs 3.
Reroll Damage	1 (Repeatable)	The Character may reroll one Challenge Dice from the current attack per Momentum spent.
Keep the Initiative	2 (Immediate)	Once per Round. Spend Momentum to activate one of your own units after the current unit's Turn is over, rather than hand play to an opponent.

A model can never leave the battlefield unless the scenario conditions specifically allow it. If a model is forced to the edge of the battlefield for any reason, the tile (battlefield) edge is treated as an impassable obstacle.

LINE OF SIGHT

Models in the same tile can see all allied and enemy models unless blocked by **Blocking Terrain** (see *Chapter 7.30: The Battlefield*, p.14). All doors are considered to be closed, and only open (and then close) to allow models to move through them.

CARRYING

An objective marker (as defined by the battle's scenario) can be carried by any Character or Squad. Place the carried marker alongside the unit that has it, and move it with the unit. Any other friendly unit can take the carried marker as a minor action in its turn. At that point the object follows the new unit. Some objectives may require a unit to have a carried object to attempt an objective Task.

If a character or squad is defeated, the objective marker is dropped and remains where it is, until another unit uses a minor action to take it. Carried objective markers can only be stolen if the carrying unit is defeated.

PRONE MODELS

In some situations, a model will be made Prone. Prone models also suffer penalties in close combat. A Prone model is laid on its side. A Prone model may perform a *Move* action to stand upright and remove its Prone status.

The *Sprint* Task is effectively 3 minor *Move* actions, and cannot be performed in the unit's same Turn as it has already performed a minor action. Therefore, the unit cannot have performed any other actions if it is to use a *Sprint* action.

MINOR ACTIONS

Minor actions are activities that do not count as a Task, and do not require dice to be rolled, such as movement. They are resolved before any Task. A unit can normally only perform one minor action each turn. However, **characters and units may spend one Momentum to make one extra minor action**, before resolving their Task. Models can never perform more than two minor actions and one Task during a turn.

The minor actions available to Characters and Squads are:

- **Aim:** The unit may reroll a single D20 made as part of a ranged attack Task in the same Turn.

- **Move:** The character moves to an adjacent zone on their tile, or through a door to a connecting zone in another tile. This minor action cannot be used if the unit then performs the *Sprint* Task. If there are one or more enemies within the unit's zone, this action cannot be performed.

Prepare: The unit prepares for, or spends time setting up, a Task. Some Tasks with some equipment require this minor action to be taken before the Task can be attempted, such as a phaser's Charge Quality.

- **Take Cover:** The unit ducks behind some cover, to gain the benefit of some Soft Cover or Hard Cover. A Cover marker must be in the same zone as the unit performing this action.

- **Take:** Take a carried marker or model, as described below.

TASKS

Tasks are activities that draw upon skill or elements of chance, such as attacking an enemy in combat. They are taken after minor actions. A unit can normally only perform one Task each Turn. The Tasks available are:

- **Melee attack:** A character or squad attacks an enemy (or another viable target) in the same zone. They use any equipped close combat weapons or unarmed skill listed under "Attacks" in their profile. This is an Opposed **Daring + Security** Task with a Difficulty of 1. See *Melee Attacks*, below (p.11).

- **Ranged attack:** A unit fires at an enemy (or other viable target) in the same tile using an equipped ranged weapon. This is a **Control + Security** Task with a Difficulty of 2. See *Ranged Attacks*, below (p.11).

- **Direct:** This Task may only be performed by the Character with the highest rank on a side. The Character nominates one friendly unit currently in play and attempts a **Control + Command** Task with a base Difficulty of 1. The nominated unit may immediately attempt a single Task ignoring the normal sequence of play. If the directed unit is in a different Tile to the character, the Difficulty is increased by 1.

- **Guard:** The unit finds some defensible position, reduces their vulnerability, or otherwise gains additional readiness for attack. This is a **Fitness + Security** Task with a Difficulty of 1, and success increases the Difficulty of any attacks (melee or ranged) made against the guarding unit by 1 until the start of the unit's next Turn.

- **First aid:** The unit targets another friendly unit in the same zone. This is a **Daring + Medicine** Task with a Difficulty of 1. Success heals a number of Stress equal to the Medicine Discipline of the model performing this Task, with an additional 1 point of Stress healed for each Momentum spent (Repeatable.) Only units with a medkit may perform this Task.

- **Operate:** This Task allows a unit to interact with objectives or other battlefield elements, such as computers or explosive devices. The scenario notes will specify which items may be operated, which Attribute and Discipline is required for the roll, the Difficulty of the Task, and the effects of success.

- **Ready:** A unit holds its fire until a more opportune target presents itself. This requires a **Control + Security** Task, with a Difficulty of 1. Place a Ready marker next to the unit. As soon as an enemy unit performs a movement action  that brings them into line of sight and range of the ready unit, the normal sequence of play is suspended. The ready unit performs a ranged attack against the new target. Once this attack is resolved, play resumes with the target unit completing its actions if it still can. Ready status lasts until a unit's next activation, and if an attack is not triggered before the unit's next activation the opportunity to attack is lost.

- **Sprint:** A unit moves quickly to cover as much ground as possible without worrying about evading enemy attention. The unit moves into any zone within 3 zones of its current location. This Task cannot be performed if the unit has carried out a minor action this Turn.

- **Fall Back:** This Task is performed if a unit is moving out of a zone that contains enemy models. This is a **Fitness + Security** Task, with a Difficulty equal to the number of enemy models engaged minus the number of friendly models. If the *Fall Back* Task succeeds, move the unit one zone. This move may not take the moving unit into another zone that contains enemy models. If the Task roll fails, one enemy unit in the same zone (chosen by the opponent) may immediately make a free melee attack against the retreating unit, before it moves one zone.

TASK DIFFICULTY

The difficulty of a Task can be altered by many factors. The maximum Difficulty of an achievable Task requires 5 successes, while the minimum is 0.

If a Task has a Difficulty of 6 or more it is impossible, and the Task cannot be attempted.

If the Task is Difficulty 0, any attempt to carry out the Task is automatically successful. and no dice are rolled. This means no Momentum can be gained for "extra" successes.

MELEE ATTACKS

Melee combat can occur when opposing units are in the same zone as one another. On their Turn, a unit that is activated while in the same zone as an enemy may perform a melee attack. The unit attempts an Opposed **Daring + Security Task** with a Difficulty of 1. If the attack is successful, then the attacker inflicts damage, as described in *Damage*, below.

ATTACKING PRONE ENEMIES

If the enemy unit that you are attacking is Prone reduce the Difficulty of the Attack by 1, to a minimum of 0.

RANGED ATTACKS

To perform a ranged attack Task, a unit must first nominate a target within the same tile. This is a **Control + Security Task** with a Difficulty of 2. If the attack is successful, then the attacker inflicts damage, as described in *Damage,* below.

RESISTANCE

Resistance is a measure of a unit's ability to shrug off damage using protective gear, innate resilience or cover. **Static Resistance** is noted on a unit's profile as a numerical value. This value is deducted from an attack's damage before the target unit's Stress is reduced. **Cover dice** can grant Resistance, but are more random, granting either 1 or 2 points of Resistance with each attack. Again, this value is deducted from the attack's overall damage before the unit's Stress is affected. Resistance may mean that a successful attack actually inflicts no damage at all.

DAMAGE

Whenever an attack is successful, it reduces the target's Stress by the weapon's or effect's **damage rating**, which will be a number of Challenge Dice, or $\blacktriangle$, with the total rolled applied against the targeted unit.

Example: *Phaser Type-2 (Ranged, 6$\blacktriangle$, Size 1H, Charge)*

In this example anyone firing a type-2 phaser would roll six Challenge Dice to check how much damage has been inflicted.

The same damage procedure is used for environmental effects if these are a feature of a battle.

Units have a quantity of **Stress**, representing their ability to withstand damage. This is the unit's **Fitness + Security**. Damage is deducted from Stress, and if the unit's Stress is reduced to 0 or less the unit is removed from the game.

1. TARGET A UNIT

- Check that the enemy unit can be targeted
- Decide whether the attack is melee (same zone) or ranged (same tile)

2. ATTEMPT A TASK

- For a ranged attack **Control + Security** with a Difficulty of 2
- For a melee attack an Opposed **Daring + Security** Task with a Difficulty of 1

3. ROLL DAMAGE IF THE ATTACK SUCCEEDS

- Roll $\blacktriangle$ based on the attack's rating: the weapon's Damage Rating + unit's Security Discipline
- Total the damage, including any Damage Effects

4. REDUCE THE DAMAGE BASED ON RESISTANCE

- Reduce the damage based on any static Resistance
- Reduce the damage based on any Cover dice rolled

5. DEDUCT REMAINING DAMAGE FROM THE TARGETED UNIT'S STRESS

- If the unit's Stress is reduced to 0, it is injured and taken out of play

DAMAGE EFFECTS

The following Damage Effects provide additional benefits for the attacker whenever an Effect is rolled on a Challenge Dice:

- **Area:** The attack affects an additional enemy model per Effect rolled, in the same zone. Apply the total damage rolled to every model simultaneously.

- **Knockdown:** A model is knocked Prone for each Effect rolled.

- **Piercing X:** The attack ignores X points of Resistance for each Effect rolled.

- **Vicious X:** The attack inflicts X additional damage for each Effect rolled.

SQUADS

SQUAD STRESS

Each model in a Squad has Stress equal to the Squad's **Security** Discipline +1 (in this case not adding its **Fitness** Attribute). Attacks against Squads are resolved in the following way:

- Reduce the total damage rolled by the unit's Resistance, either from its static Resistance or Cover dice.

  - Divide the remaining damage by the Stress of each model, and remove that many models from play.

  - Any "left over" damage is lost.

Example: *A Klingon warband has 5 members in it. They are Klingon warriors, so their Security Discipline is 2. Each model's Stress is 3, and their 5 members gives the unit a total Stress of 15.*

If this Klingon warband is shot at and takes 7 damage after Resistance and Cover are taken into account, they will lose 2 models from the squad because 7/3 = 2 with remainder 1. The 1 damage is ignored.

STRENGTH IN NUMBERS

Squads gain bonus D20s and bonus Challenge Dice ▲ to their Task and damage rolls based on their current head count, as shown:

SQUAD BONUS DICE

NUMBER OF MODELS	DEFAULT TASK ROLL	BONUS CHALLENGE DICE
2-4	3d20	+1 ▲
5-6	4d20	+2 ▲
7-10	5d20	+3 ▲

Remember, no more than 5D20 can ever be rolled at once for a Task.

RED ALERT
STARTING A GAME

SETTING UP

Each game that you play represents a conflict between two or more opposing sides, with the aim to complete one or more objectives to determine a winner. For this reason, *Star Trek Adventures: Red Alert* is structured around scenarios, which provide a variety of gaming set-ups, special deployments and victory conditions to keep each battle fresh and challenging.

ASSEMBLING THE TEAM

Teams are comprised of Characters and Squads, each with their own **Force Value.** Their Force Value is equal to their combined Stress + Security Discipline values. For a Squad's Force Value, multiply a single model's stress by the number of models in the Squad, then add the Security Discipline of the unit.

- **Character Force Value** = Stress + Security
- **Squad Force Value** = (Stress × No. of models) + Security

When assembling their sides, players should agree on a maximum value and not exceed this. With an average Force Value of 15 for each Character or Squad, the following limits should be used as guidelines:

- **Force Value 30** = 2 units
- **Force Value 60** = 4 units
- **Force Value 90** = 6 units

If one player's Force Value is less than the other, they automatically take the first Turn in the first Round, instead of rolling to determine initiative.

For Gamemasters who are using these rules as part of a roleplay campaign, points values often aren't required, except perhaps as balancing factors. Gamemasters are encouraged to plan their encounters and then manipulate the scenario criteria and objectives as they see fit.

ESCALATION

Whenever a unit has a weapon listed with an **Escalation** cost, a player may give 2 Momentum to an opposing player at the start of the game to upgrade the attacks of a single unit. This cost is separate for each unit, but grants them access to all their Escalation attacks (therefore for two units to gain access to all their attacks with an Escalation cost, that player must give 4 Momentum to their opponent during Set Up. This Momentum is available during the first *Establish Initiative* step in the *Sequence of Play*, below.

THE BATTLEFIELD

To begin with, set up your tiles (or custom game board) as specified by the scenario. Place any objective or Cover markers, these before setting up your miniatures.

COVER

Any artwork on the tiles that is deemed as Cover by the scenario need a **Cover token** placed on it. Tokens can be found at the end of this chapter.

DEPLOYMENT

Once everything is set up and ready, deploy your forces as described in the scenario rules. Once this is done, you're ready to do battle!

SEQUENCE OF PLAY

Each game is divided into **Rounds** and **Turns**. A Round represents the period of time in which all models on the table have taken actions during their Turn. Once all models have acted the Round ends and a new Round begins. A Turn represents a Player taking a minor action and a Task with one of their Characters or Squads.

Each Round follows a strict sequence, as follows:

1. **Establish Initiative**
2. **Activate Models**
3. **Tidy up the Battlefield**

1. ESTABLISH INITIATIVE

At the start of each Round, the Character with the highest rank of each side, as noted on their profile, **attempts an Opposed Daring + Command Task** with a Difficulty of 0. Any successes that remain for the Player who won the Opposed Task, after comparing, generates Momentum as normal.

In the first Round of the game, ties must be resolved — if no winner is determined, roll again until a clear winner is found. **The winner of the roll gains the Initiative for the Round**.

In the event of a tie in the second and subsequent Rounds, the Initiative always goes to the player who didn't have it in the previous Round.

In the case of a game with more than two players, the Initiative order follows the number of successes each player scored from highest to lowest. In the case of ties, roll again for the Players who are tied. After this, if the Player with the first Turn had any excess successes, they generate Momentum as normal.

2. ACTIVATE MODELS

The Player with the Initiative activates one Character or Squad that has not yet been activated this Round. The unit completes a minor action and a Task, and then the current Player hands play over to the next Player in the Initative order. Repeat this step until all Players have activated all of their units.

3. TIDY UP THE BATTLEFIELD

At the end of each Round, Players should check the victory conditions of the scenario they are playing. If these have been met, the game ends. If not, Players should remove any markers or tokens that are not currently applicable. A new Round then begins by once more rolling for Initiative.

RED ALERT
THE BATTLEFIELD

TERRAIN

On the **Star Trek Adventures** tile sets consoles, tables, chairs and other objects are laid out over the scene. Scenarios will denote which zones contain Cover.

BLOCKING TERRAIN

Black areas of the tile sets, usually around the edges or within thick walls block line of site, are blocking terrain. Attacks cannot target units with blocking terrain between the attacking and defending units.

COVER

There are two types of Cover in Star Trek Adventures: Red Alert, soft and hard. If a targeted unit has performed the Take Cover minor action then Cover provides a number of ⬧ of Resistance to incoming attacks. Cover dice apply against any attacks targeting a unit in Cover.

- **Soft Cover** provides 1⬧ of Resistance
- **Cover** provides 2⬧ of Resistance

Cover dice are rolled after the attack's damage is determined but before damage is applied, as in *Attacks,* above (p.11).

OBJECTIVE MARKERS

Some missions use objective markers, a token on the table that represents a point of interest or object that models need to interact with. Each mission will define how an objective token works on the table. You can find soft cover, hard cover, and objective tokens at the end of this book.

DOORS

Doors can be passed through freely as part of a movement action. All doors are otherwise closed and block line of sight. If a door is marked on the boundary of a tile then the adjoining tile must contain a matching door, or be completely open in order for the door to be used. If an adjoining tile has a solid wall where the door should be, models may not pass through the door.

RED ALERT BATTLEFIELD TOKENS

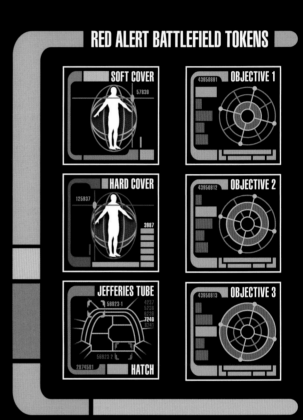

JEFFERIES TUBES

Hatches and Jefferies tubes may connect to other locations around the tile map laid out for a mission. As such, markers will be placed showing where these maintenance ducts can be entered and exited. The rules for attacks, line of sight and zones still apply to these maintenance areas, but a Sprint action cannot be performed due to the cramped conditions.

TURBOLIFTS

The turbolift system is a key infrastructure element aboard starships and other installations, that can deliver crew to any deck or location. Units starting their Turn in a turbolift can perform a Move minor action to move from one turbolift zone to any other. Turbolifts count as a separate zone in all cases, but their doors do not block line of sight.

RED ALERT
WEAPONS AND EQUIPMENT

This section provides descriptions of a range of common items and technologies in use by Starfleet personnel and other cultures in the wider Galaxy.

WEAPON PROFILES

RANGE

Attacks with the 'Melee' range can only be used to perform melee attacks in the same zone. If the range is 'Ranged' then units in the same tile may be targeted.

DAMAGE RATING

This is the number of Challenge Dice ▲ the weapon rolls when making an attack, and the result is the damage it inflicts.

DAMAGE EFFECTS

The following Damage Effects provide additional benefits for the attacker whenever an Effect is rolled on a Challenge Dice:

- **Area:** The attack affects an additional target model per Effect rolled, in the same zone. Apply the total damage rolled to every model simultaneously.

- **Knockdown:** A model is knocked Prone for each Effect rolled.

- **Piercing X:** The attack ignores X points of Resistance for each Effect rolled.

- **Vicious X:** The attack inflicts X additional damage for each Effect rolled.

QUALITIES

A weapon's Qualities are special rules that alter the way the weapon functions, either by applying bonuses or restrictions. In the Weapons Reference Table these Qualities are listed as keywords.

- **Accurate:** This weapon is precise, incorporating sights and other targeting equipment. If the unit performs the *Aim* minor action before attacking with this weapon, they may reroll any number of d20s during their Task attempt.

- **Charge:** The weapon has an adaptable energy supply. If the unit performed the *Prepare* minor action before attacking with this weapon, they can choose to apply one of the following Damage Effects: Area, Piercing 2, or Vicious 1.

WEAPON REFERENCE CHART

The most common forms of weapons in the game are listed on the chart below. Alien profiles, or profiles of units from different eras of the Federation, will differ from this list.

A unit's attack damage for each weapon is a number of Challenge Dice ▲ equal to the weapon's Damage Rating plus the unit's Security Discipline.

NAME	TYPE	DAMAGE RATING	QUALITIES	COST
Unarmed Strike	Melee	1▲ Knockdown	Nonlethal	–
Knife/Dagger	Melee	1▲ Vicious 1	Deadly, Hidden 1	Opportunity 1
Blade (sword, *mek'leth*, etc)	Melee	2▲ Vicious 1	–	Opportunity 1
Heavy Blade (*bat'leth, kar'takin, lirpa*)	Melee	3▲ Vicious 1	–	Opportunity 1, Escalation 1
Phaser Type-1	Ranged	2▲	Charge, Hidden 1	Standard Issue
Phaser Type-2	Ranged	3▲	Charge	Standard Issue
Phaser Type-3 (phaser rifle)	Ranged	4▲	Accurate, Charge	Opportunity 1, Escalation 2
Pulse Grenade	Ranged	4▲ Area	Charge, Grenade	Opportunity 1, Escalation 2
Disruptor Pistol	Ranged	3▲ Vicious 1	–	Not Available
Disruptor Rifle	Ranged	4▲ Vicious 1	Accurate	Not Available

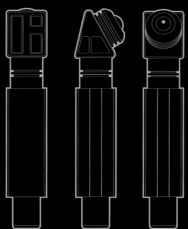

- **Cumbersome:** The weapon cannot be used to attack unless the *Prepare* minor action was performed before the attack.

- **Debilitating:** Medicine Tasks to perform *First Aid* on units affected by this weapon have their Difficulty increased by 1.

- **Grenade:** This weapon is a thrown explosive device. A unit normally carries enough grenades for 3 grenade attacks in one battle.

- **Inaccurate:** Units attacking with this weapon cannot benefit from the *Aim* minor action.

OTHER EQUIPMENT

MEDKIT
A character or unit equipped with a medkit can perform the *First Aid* Task.

MULTI-TOOL
A character with a multi-tool reduces the Difficulty of any *Operate* Task by 1.

TRICORDER
Units may need a tricorder in order to complete certain Tasks, such as *Operate*, or other Tasks required by a scenario.

SETTING UP

Pick a scenario, a conflict between two or more sides.

Each Player chooses a force. This is team of **units**, with **Characters** and **Squads.** All units have a **Force Value**, and the units on a side cannot add up to more than a **total Force Value** agreed between the Players for the battle. Each Character and Squad member needs a **model** to represent them.

Set up the battlefield using tiles. Tiles have zones to provide separate areas for models to occupy and move through.

Each Player places their models on the battlefield following the scenario instructions and the general deployment rules.

THE BATTLE

Battles are divided into **Rounds** and **Turns**. The game ends when only one side has units left, or when a Player completes all their objectives.

There can be many Turns each Round: one for each unit, in fact. Once every unit has had a Turn the current Round ends, and a new begins.

Each Round follows a simple sequence:

1. ESTABLISH INITIATIVE

Each player rolls to see if their side acts first. The abilities of the Character with the highest in-game rank are used for this Task, even if that Character isn't the best leader on their side.

2. ACTIVATE MODELS IN TURN

The Player with the initiative may now choose one unit and have it do a **minor action** and a **Task**, in that order.

- **Minor actions** are simple things, and will always succeed. Aiming a weapon, moving or taking cover are typical minor actions.

- **Tasks** are more difficult things, and the unit will have to make a successful dice roll to carry out the Task. **Melee Attack** and **Ranged Attack** are the two most important Tasks. The results of any Task are applied immediately. An attack, for example, may well wipe out an enemy unit before it has chance to act.

When a unit has finished a Task another Player then has the chance to act with one of their units. This alternating activation continues until every unit has had a Turn.

3. TIDY UP THE BATTLEFIELD

When every Turn has been taken, a Round ends. Tokens that are no longer needed are removed. Check to see if the scenario victory conditions have been completed and, if they have, the winner is declared. Otherwise, initiative is determined for the next Round.

RESOLVING AN ATTACK
87-1

1. TARGET A UNIT
- Check that the enemy unit can be targeted
- Decide whether the attack is melee (same zone) or ranged (same tile)

2. ATTEMPT A TASK
- For a ranged attack **Control + Security** with a Difficulty of 2
- For a melee attack an Opposed **Daring + Security** with a Difficulty of 1

3. ROLL DAMAGE IF THE ATTACK SUCCEEDS
- Roll ▲ based on the attack's rating: the weapon's Damage Rating + unit's Security Discipline
- Total the damage, including any Damage Effects

4. REDUCE THE DAMAGE BASED ON RESISTANCE
- Reduce the damage based on any static Resistance
- Reduce the damage based on any Cover dice rolled

5. DEDUCT REMAINING DAMAGE FROM THE TARGETED UNIT'S STRESS
- If the model's Stress is reduced to 0, it is injured and taken out of play

MOMENTUM SPENDS
66-3498   67-3498

SPEND	COST	EFFECT
Create Opportunity	1+ (Immediate, Repeatable)	Buy extra d20 to roll before attempting a Task. The first die bought costs 1, the second die bought costs 2, the third die bought costs 3.
Reroll Damage	1 (Repeatable)	The Character may reroll one Challenge Dice from the current attack per Momentum spent.
Keep the Initiative	2 (Immediate)	Once per Round. Spend Momentum to activate one of your own units as soon as this character's Turn is over, rather than hand play to an opponent.

32-6   17-9   24-5   76-2   76-4   27-8   98-1

RED ALERT
MISSIONS

BRIEFING

These missions provide a short *Red Alert* campaign, and introduce varying sizes of mission as it progresses. You'll need a set of *Next Generation* and Klingon miniatures, as well as the *Starfleet Deck Tiles* set, in order to play.

OBJECTIVES

Key words are used in the following missions as a shorthand to describe the victory conditions for the two sides:

- **Defeat:** Reduce a Character, Squad, or a whole force, to 0 Stress.

- **Steal:** Succeed at a **Daring + Security Task** with a Difficulty of 3.

- **Sabotage:** Succeed at a **Control + Engineering Task** with a Difficulty of 2.

- **Repair:** Succeed at a **Control + Engineering Task** with a Difficulty of 4.

- **Program:** Succeed at a **Control + Conn Task** with a Difficulty of 3.

- **Occupy:** Have a unit present in a particular zone, without an enemy unit in the same zone.

Lt. Commander Worf is enjoying a glass of prune juice, alone at a table, trying to avoid the Klingon diplomatic contingent who have come aboard with bodyguards. Unfortunately, one of the Klingon warriors incites her friends, "Look at this poor excuse for a warrior! He is not even a warrior, he is a P'takh! Let's show it what we do to those without honor!"

Worf knocks her to the floor, rendering her unconscious, but 3 more Klingons square up to him. Now he must defend himself as the door to Ten Forward locks to contain the fight!

SET UP

- **Ten Forward tile**
- **3 Klingon warriors (squad) [K]**
- **Worf [W]**

OBJECTIVES

- **Klingons** must **defeat** Worf
- **Worf** must **defeat** the Klingons

SPECIAL RULES

- Only unarmed strikes may be used as attacks.
- This mission teaches you the basics of moving, attacking, and damage. If you wish, you may stop this mission at the end of Round 3, with the Player with the most Stress remaining in their force declared the winner.

WORF VICTORY

If Worf wins, move to *Mission 2: Armory*.

KLINGON VICTORY

If the Klingons win, move to *Mission 3: Shuttlebay*.

Commander Riker is reviewing an armory report, when Commander Troi walks in. "My shift's just finished, and if I'm not mistaken, so has yours. Now, it's my professional opinion as ship's counsellor that you need to take a break." Their moment is rudely interrupted, however, by a squad of Klingon warriors looking to raid the weapons from the armory!

SET UP

- **Armory tile, two generic corridor tiles**
- **5 Klingon warriors (squad) [K], 1 Klingon Veteran [V]**
- **Riker [R[, Troi [T]**

OBJECTIVES

- **Klingons** must **steal** weapons in the armory room [1] and at least one model who took part in the Task leave via the turbolifts.
- **Starfleet** must **sabotage** the weapons in the armory room (marked) to disable them, or **defeat** the Klingons.

SPECIAL RULES

- Players may not purchase weapons using the Escalation rules.

STARFLEET VICTORY

If Starfleet wins, move to *Mission 4: Battlebridge*.

KLINGON VICTORY

If the Klingons win, move to *Mission 5: Main Engineering*.

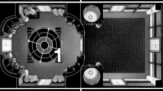

The red alert klaxon echoes around the shuttlebay, as Door 3 crunches under the impact of a Klingon boarding party. Lieutenant Commander Geordi La Forge and Lieutenant Commander Data have been assigned to secure the breach.

SET UP

- Shuttlebay tiles, pictured
- 5 Klingon warriors (squad) [K], 1 Klingon veteran [V]
- Geordi La Forge [G], Data [D]

OBJECTIVES

- **Klingons** must **sabotage** the *Enterprise's* shields [2] to allow boarding parties to beam aboard.
- **Starfleet** must **repair** the shuttlebay doors [1] to close the breach.

SPECIAL RULES

- The Klingon Player may spawn a Squad of 3 Klingon warriors at the shuttlebay door (marked as the Starfleet objective) by spending 3 Momentum, once per mission.

STARFLEET VICTORY

If Starfleet wins, move to *Mission 4: Battle Bridge*.

KLINGON VICTORY

If the Klingons win, move to *Mission 6: The Bridge*.

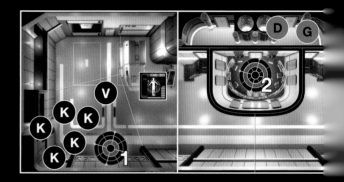

Under orders of Captain Picard, the saucer section is to be separated to cut the Klingon boarders off from their commander. It's up to Commander Riker, Commander Crusher, Lt. Commander La Forge, and Lt. Worf to get to the Battle Bridge to initiate separation! The Klingons have different plans…

SET UP

- Battle Bridge tile, round service area tile, generic tiles
- 5 Klingon warriors (squad) [K], 3 Klingon veterans [V]
- Riker [R], Crusher [C], Troi [T], La Forge [G], Worf [W]

OBJECTIVES

- **A Klingon** veteran must **carry** the objective marker to the Battle Bridge zone [1] and **sabotage** the Battle Bridge [1].
- **Starfleet** must **program** a saucer separation on the Battle Bridge zone [1] before it is sabotaged.

SPECIAL RULES

- The Klingon Player may spawn one Klingon warrior from a door on the outer edge of the map by spending 1 Momentum (Immediate, Repeatable).
- The Klingon player may not give their opponent Momentum for Escalation spends to upgrade their weapons.
- Turbolifts cannot be used.

STARFLEET VICTORY

Captain Picard and his crew have successfully repelled the Klingon attack, and diplomatic negotiations may be resumed once Commander Moq'var and his crew are transferred back to the Klingon Defense Force from the *Enterprise* brig. The *Enterprise* has saved these diplomatic talks, and maintained relations with the Klingon Empire for the better.

KLINGON VICTORY

Commander Moq'var has taken nominal control of the *Enterprise* but doesn't have access to fly her anywhere. With both Federation and Klingon ships approaching the *Enterprise*, who knows what will happen! Moq'var can only hope the Klingons arrive first!

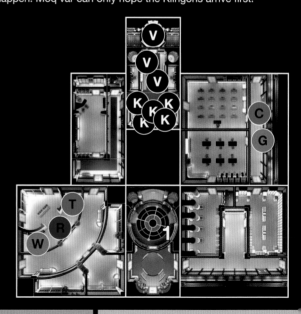

...# MISSION 5: ENGINEERING

With the Enterprise under attack, diplomatic talks with the Klingon general have broken down, and to save his ship Captain Picard must get to main engineering to lock out the Klingons from accessing the controls to the Enterprise.

SET UP

- Main engineering tiles, nacelle systems operations tile, sensor maintenance room tile, the Jefferies tube junction tile
- 3 Klingon warriors (squad) [K], 3 Klingon warriors (squad) [K], 2 Klingon veterans [V]
- Picard [P], Data [D], Crusher [C], Worf [W], La Forge [G]

OBJECTIVES

- A Klingon veteran must sabotage both the warp core [1] and the warp nacelles [2].
- Starfleet must occupy main engineering [1], and Picard must sabotage the controls of the Enterprise [2].

SPECIAL RULES

- If the Klingons succeeded at *Mission 2: Armory*, the Klingon player may give their models phaser type-3 rifles by paying the Escalation cost.
- (Either) If Starfleet succeeded at *Mission 3: The Shuttleba* the Klingon player may not spend Momentum to bring in reinforcements, disregarding the next special rule from th mission.
- (Or) The Klingon player may spawn a Squad of 3 Klingon warriors from a Jefferies tube hatch by spending 3 Mome (Immediate), once per mission.

STARFLEET VICTORY

If Starfleet locks out the *Enterprise* controls, they have cont the Klingon insurrection, but are unable to navigate the ship to receive help. With both Federation and Klingon fleets on intercept course, Picard's only hope is that his crew can hol until then… unless the Klingon fleet arrives first.

KLINGON VICTORY

If the Klingons win, Commander Moq'var has taken nominal of the *Enterprise* but doesn't have access to fly her anywhere both Federation and Klingon ships inbound on the *Enterprise* location, who knows what will happen. Moq'var can only hop Klingons arrive first!

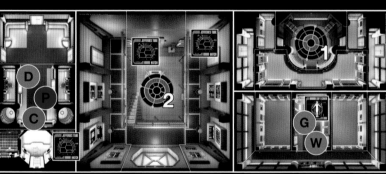

12-17032
13-17033

19-3300		21-5540		12-3788	17
39366298	29842I	553058	229451	455295	27383937
83769145	7678	176876	57862	868251	78293791
20343360	320901	236103	15032	273029	24730282
24369201	843920	175073	234921	138430	11239403
24994020	3892	23392	107052	193402	17394550
23892680	48628	568299	56854	836191	48571858

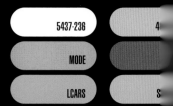

976243	92435629	9	314798	•	17546	48749	4169122	971233	419848		4896	498	325	78	314124
395879	27865293	7	949357	•	38591	26874	3692397	297599	994825	287499	614	193	2229	434392
836501	12971240	5	294981	•	48917	14810	4828759	937581	313949		198	97	291	186	936221
563478	24536852	3	534780	•	62398	92834	2377246	586899	645921		4572	452	2547	8457	825417

04-248248

5437-236

MODE

LCARS

SEARCH

MISSION 6: THE BRIDGE

With the Klingons beaming aboard the Enterprise *on every deck, Commander Moq'var can now launch his final attack on the bridge, gaining control of the ship! But the crew of the* Enterprise *must stand their ground in the line of duty.*

SET UP

- Bridge tile, transporter room tile, sensor maintenance room tile, crew quarters tile, Jefferies tube junction tile
- 4 Klingon warriors (squad) [K], 4 Klingon warriors (squad) [K], 1 Klingon veteran [V], Moq'var Son of Koloth [M]
- Picard [P], Riker [R], Troi [T], Data [D], Worf [W]

OBJECTIVES

- The Klingons must **occupy** the bridge and **program** an override at the captain's chair [1] to take control of the ship.
- **Starfleet** must **occupy** the transporter room [2] and **defeat** Moq'var Son of Koloth [M].

SPECIAL RULES

- The Klingon Player may spawn a Squad of 3 Klingon war in the transporter room by spending 3 Momentum (Imme once per mission.
- The Klingon Player may spend 2 extra Momentum when spawning a Klingon Squad to place it anywhere on the map

STARFLEET VICTORY

If Starfleet defeats Moq'var and takes the transporter room b they have contained the Klingon insurrection but are unable navigate the ship to get help. With both Federation and Kling fleets on an intercept course, Picard must hope his crew can out, as long as the Klingon fleet arrives after Starfleet.

KLINGON VICTORY

If Moq'var takes control of the *Enterprise*, the Klingon Empire has taken control of the Federation's flagship! A victory worth the Hall of Heroes! Moq'var immediately orders the *Enterpris* Qo'noS, taking his prize back to the heart of the Empire.

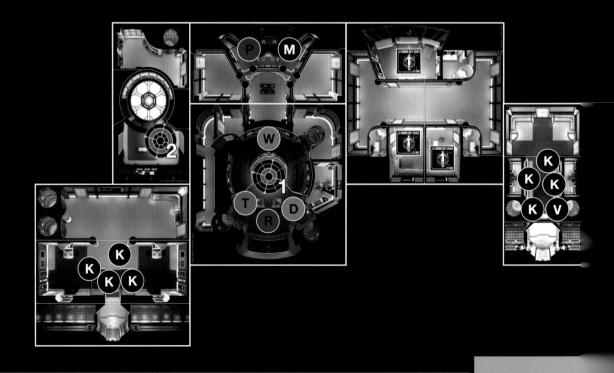

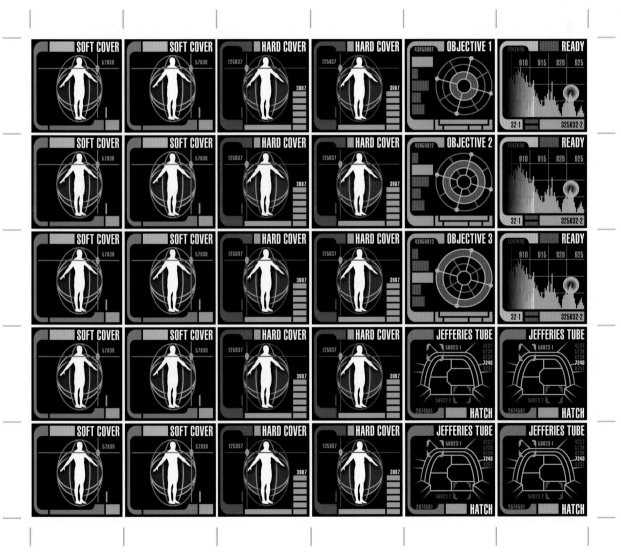

™ & © 2018 CBS Studios Inc. STAR TREK and related marks and logos are trademarks of CBS Studios Inc. All Rights Reserved.
Permission granted to reproduce for personal use.

Advanced Starship Design Bureau 11-12
Ahwahnee, U.S.S. 27
Al-Khaled, Lt. Commander Mahmud 89
Alien Technologies.......................................81
Anbo-jutsu..73
Andorian 36, 73, 94
Android 62-64
Antideuterium 5, 61
Antimatter........................ 5, 11, 25, 56, 60-61
Antineutrinos 61
Archer, Captain Jonathan.......................10, 14
Archer, Henry...4, 75
Archives, Starfleet Intelligence 19
Armory Officer 4
Arrest...71
Assistance with Civilian Projects..................25
Attacks...105
Away Team Security Protocols......................69
Away Teams in the Enterprise &
    Original Series Eras...............................68
Bajoran 36, 40, 76, 94
Basic Principles.................................. 98-101
Benevolent, U.S.S. 52
Bilana III...63
Blue Plot Components 67, 76
    ◖ Engineering...................................... 76-79
    ◖ Security 67-68
Borg Collective, the............ 6-7, 11, 19, 27, 33,
                                        55, 64, 74, 98
Brahms, Dr. Leah..................................88-89
Breen..36
Cardassian 6, 16, 19-20, 29, 32,
                            34, 36, 41, 44, 68, 76
Cardassian Affairs Section 19
Challenge Dice 99
Characters...99
Chief of Starfleet Intelligence 17-18
Cochrane, Zefram 4
Collection & Analysis of Evidence 70
Combat Engineer 38
Common Engineering Tools 54-57
Communications Officer...............................92
Corps of Engineers History 27
Corps of Engineers in play 27-28
Corps of Engineers Organization &
    Deployment...23
Covert Agents..18
Creating Engineering Characters 46
Creating Security Characters 40
Crime and the Prime Directive.....................67
Criminal Investigation 70-71

Cultural Observation Support.......................26
Cutting Tools 54-55
Damage Control Revisited...........................82
Dax, Jadzia...45
Daystrom Institute 61, 88
Daystrom, Dr. Richard 61-62
Deep Space 9...6
Deniable Asset, A 32
Derelict Recovery 78
Derived Statistics 100-101
Design Flexibility...58
Deuterium 60-61
Diagnostics (Level 1-5)................................81
Dilithium...52, 61
Disaster Relief 24-25
Distress Call Response 25
Doctor, The................................24, 49, 84
Dominion War..36
Dominion, The 16, 36
Earth-Romulan War.....................................36
Engineering Focuses 49-51
    ◖ Advanced Holograms........................49
    ◖ Cybernetics 49
    ◖ Diagnostics......................................50
    ◖ Electro-Plasma Systems 50
    ◖ Emergency Repairs 50
    ◖ Energy Weapons 50
    ◖ Flight Control Systems.......................50
    ◖ Imaging Equipment 50
    ◖ Impulse Fundamentals 50
    ◖ Jury-Rigging 50
    ◖ Modeling & Design 50
    ◖ Reverse Engineering..........................50
    ◖ Sensor Calibration............................50
    ◖ Structural Engineering 50
    ◖ System Maintenance.........................50
    ◖ Transporters/Replicators 50
    ◖ Troubleshooting................................50
    ◖ Warp Core Mechanics........................51
Engineering in Play................................ 47-48
Engineering Specialist 91
Engineering Talents 51-52
    ◖ Experimental Device.........................51
    ◖ Exploit Engineering Flaw 51
    ◖ Maintenance Specialist 51
    ◖ Meticulous.......................................51
    ◖ Miracle Worker 52
    ◖ Past the Redline 52
    ◖ Procedural Compliance......................52
    ◖ Repair Team Leader 52
    ◖ Right tool for the right job 52

◖ Rocks into Replicators 52
Engineering Tricorder 54
Enlisted Crewman 37
Enlisted Security Training.............................37
Enterprise, NX-01.. 12-13, 16, 39, 41, 68, 76, 95
Enterprise, U.S.S.......4, 6, 13, 16, 26, 39, 41, 49,
            62-63, 68, 72, 74, 76, 87, 95, 114-116
Episodes Focused on Engineering
    Challenges 76
Episodes Focused on Security Challenges...68
EPS (electro-plasma system) conduits 27, 50,
    56, 58, 61, 82, 91
Excelsior, U.S.S. 13, 64
Experimental Technology,
    Starfleet Intelligence 19
Explosive Ordnance Expert..........................38
Federation Security Section 19
Federation-Cardassian War..........................36
Federation-Klingon War...............................36
Federation-Tzenkethi War 36
Field Destabilizers 55-56
Field Medic...39
Fire at Will Talent 43
First Contact.......................................67, 75
Flag Officers in Play....................................88
Fleet Operations............................... 10-15, 25
Fleet Operations in Play 14
Fleet Operations in the 22nd & 23rd Century.... 14
Fleet Operations Organisation Structure...13-14
Forensic Autopsy.................................. 70-71
Formal Scientists..77
Gelling 6 20
Genesis...24, 27
Giertz, Commander Simone.........................24
Gold Plot Components............... 71-72, 79-80
    ◖ Engineering......................................79
    ◖ Security 71
Grappling Styles...73
Graves, Dr Ira. 63-64
Harriman, Admiral John...........................87-88
Hazardous Materials....................................82
Heavy Weapons Specialist 39
Helm & Navigator 74
Hyperspanner...56
Immobilize Task..73
Infiltration..20
Informant (NPC)..86
Internal Systems Control (Tactical)...............74
Investigation of Alien Technologies (SCE) 24
Investigative Agents 18
Ja'Dar, Dr..63

Joining Starfleet Intelligence 21-22
Judge Advocate General Office 13
Jury-rigged Devices 57
Keevan...23
Kiev, U.S.S. 5
Kim, Ensign Harry.................................45, 49
Kirk, Rear Admiral James T. .. 11, 13-14, 87, 98
Klingon 19, 27, 31, 33, 36, 39, 44,
       72-73, 92, 98-101, 106, 112-116
Klingon Affairs Section 19
La Forge, Lt. Commander Geordi 49, 54
Laren, Ensign Ro 41
Lasers 54
Life Scientists 77
M-5 Multitronic Unit..............................61-62
MACO
    (Military Assault Command Operations) ...39
MACO Soldier 95-96
Magnetic Probe 58
Managing Defections 20
Maquis...18, 20, 76
Marcus, Doctor...................................24, 27
Micro-optic Drill..54
Miniature Scale...100
Mission Operations 10
Mission Operations in play.....................14-15
Models...99
Mok'bara 73
Momentum 102
Momentum Spends..........................102, 111
Nerys, Major Kira...40
Non-Lethal Attack 73
O'Brien, Chief Petty Officer Miles.... 5-6, 41, 45
Objective 114
Obsidian Order 16-18, 22, 32
Operations Department................................45
Operations Officer 92
Operations, Starfleet Intelligence 19-21
Opposed Task 101
Other Equipment 110
Pegasus, U.S.S.......................16-17, 19, 21, 62
Periods of Conflict.......................................36
Phaser Drill 54
Phasing Cloak 62
Physical Scientists.......................................77
Picard, Captain Jean-Luc.............. 72, 114-116
Planetary Scientists.....................................77
Plasma Torch 54
Plating, Gravity.....................................58, 78
Playing Security Campaigns 39
Pressman, Rear Admiral Erik.......................16
Profiles..100
Project Profiles 23-25
Quartermaster 90
Raner, Admiral 84
Reconnaissance 39
Recruited to Starfleet Intelligence,
    Career Event 21
Red Alert Missions 113-116
    ● Mission 1: Bar Brawl 113
    ● Mission 2: Armory.............................113
    ● Mission 3: Shuttlebay.....................114

● Mission 4: Battle Bridge 114
● Mission 5: Engineering 115
● Mission 6: The Bridge.........................116
Red Alert Rules Summary 111
Red Alert Tokens 117
Red Plot Components...........................86, 75
    ● Security Department 86
    ● Engineering Department.......................75
Redirect Task 73
Regula 24
Repair Team Leader 92-93
Replicator 6, 8, 10, 23, 46, 50, 52, 56-57,
       59-60, 63, 72, 77, 79, 80-81, 91
Replicator Ethics 59
Right Tools, The...54
Riker, Commander William 40, 101,
       113-114, 116
Romulan 16-17, 19-20, 22, 27, 29, 31-32,
       36, 44, 62, 68, 76, 85, 87-88, 98
Romulan Affairs Section 19
Romulus 20, 70, 77
Rutledge, U.S.S. 6
Salvage...26
SCE Safety Regulations 26
Science Operations 10
Scott, Lt. Commander Montgomery ... 4, 58-59
Section 31 .... 19, 29-34
    ● History and Organization...............30-31
    ● Section 31 Operations...................31-32
Security Focuses 42
    ● Criminal Organizations 42
    ● Fleet Formations.................................42
    ● Forensics 42
    ● Hazardous Environments 42
    ● Martial Arts 42
    ● Small Unit Tactics...............................42
    ● Ship Engagement Tactics....................42
    ● Ship Lockdown Procedures..................42
    ● Security Systems................................42
    ● Targeting Systems...............................42
Security in Play...................................... 39-40
Security Talents 42-43
    ● Combat Medic.....................................42
    ● Criminal Minds 42-43
    ● Crisis Management 43
    ● Deadeye Marksman 43
    ● Full Spread – Maximum Yield!..............43
    ● Heavy Cover 43
    ● Lead Investigator................................43
    ● Martial Artist 43
    ● Precision Targeting.............................43
Sequence of Play 107
Setting Up 106-107
Shipyards Operations............. 10, 11, 12-13, 15
Shran, Ensign 56
Sloan, Luther 29, 32, 85-86
Soliton Wave Generator 63
Son'a 36
Sonic Driver 56
Soong, Dr Noonien...............................62-64
Spock, Ambassador.....................................20
Sprint..103

Squad Leader..38
Squads 99, 106
Starbase 24
Starbase Operations 10, 13, 15
Starfleet Command 27
Starfleet Corps of Engineers 10, 23-29,
       44-45, 81
Starfleet Engineer's Mate 95
Starfleet Engineering Campaign.............. 28-29
Starfleet Intelligence......................... 2, 16-22
    ● In Play...21
    ● Organization 17-18
Starfleet Intelligence Agent 85
Starfleet Security 37
Starfleet Security Officer 93-94
Striking Styles...73
Structural Damage 82
Suspect & Witness Interviews.......................71
Suus Mahna 73
Synaptic Scanning Technique........................63
Tactical Operations................................10-11
    ● In Play...15
Tactical Roles 38-39
Tal Shiar..16, 32
Tasks 101, 104
Technobabble...48
Temporal Investigations Interview 34
Terraforming Support, ...26
Terrain..108
Transport Inhibitor 56-57
Transporter Chief..91
Transporter Cross-section............................60
Transporters 56-57, 59-60, 63, 72, 79, 80-81, 91
Transwarp Drive...64
Treaty of Algeron 62, 76
Tucker, Commander Charles "Trip" ...49, 75, 89
Tzenkethi 36
Unarmed Combat...73
Uniforms of the Corps of Engineers..............45
Use of Psionic Abilities.................................71
Verifying Intelligence....................................20
Vulcan...16, 20
Warp Core, ...4-7, 11-12, 28-29, 37-38, 42-43,
       45, 51-52, 56, 60-61, 63, 66-67, 73,
       76-78, 81-82, 89, 93, 100-101, 115
Warp Drive.............................4, 12, 26, 50, 58,
       60-61, 63-64, 76, 78, 95
Weapon Impacts 82
Weapon Profiles 109
Weapon Reference Chart 109
Weapon-Based Styles...................................73
Wolf 359 27
Working with the Science Department...........77
Wozniak, U.S.S. 27
Xindi...36
Yesterday's Enterprise 4, 26
Zimmerman, Captain Herman 87

STAR TREK™
ADVENTURES

A FULL RANGE OF BOOKS & ACCESSORIES

NCC-1701-D Limited Edition Corebook
Away Team Edition Corebook
Command Division Book
Operations Division Book
Sciences Division Book
Alpha Quadrant Book
Beta Quadrant Book
Gamma Quadrant Book
Delta Quadrant Book
These Are The Voyages: Missions Vol.1
Limited Edition Borg Cube Box Set

Gamesmaster Screen
Command, Operations & Sciences Dice Sets
The Next Generation Miniatures
The Original Series Miniatures
Romulan Strike Team Miniatures
Klingon Warband Miniatures
Borg Collective Miniatures
Starfleet Away Team Miniatures
Star Trek Villains Miniatures
Starfleet Geomorphic Deck Tiles
Starfleet Landing Party Miniatures

AVAILABLE FROM MODIPHIUS.COM/STAR-TREK
OR VISIT YOUR FRIENDLY LOCAL GAMING STORE

MODIPHIUS™

TM & © 2018 CBS Studios Inc. STAR TREK and
related marks are trademarks of CBS Studios Inc.
All Rights Reserved.

2D20™